TO THE MARGINS

To the Margins

Pope Francis
and the Mission of the Church

Andrea Riccardi

Translated by Dinah Livingstone

ORBIS BOOKS
Maryknoll, New York 10545

Founded in 1970, Orbis Books endeavors to publish works that enlighten the mind, nourish the spirit, and challenge the conscience. The publishing arm of the Maryknoll Fathers and Brothers, Orbis seeks to explore the global dimensions of the Christian faith and mission, to invite dialogue with diverse cultures and religious traditions, and to serve the cause of reconciliation and peace. The books published reflect the views of their authors and do not represent the official position of the Maryknoll Society. To learn more about Maryknoll and Orbis Books, please visit our website at www.maryknollsociety.org.

Library of Congress Cataloging-in-Publication Data

Names: Riccardi, Andrea, 1950- author.

Title: To the margins : Pope Francis and the mission of the church / Andrea Riccardi ; translated by Dinah Livingstone.

Other titles: Periferie. English

Description: Maryknoll : Orbis Books, 2018.

Identifiers: LCCN 2017040789 (print) | LCCN 2017048559 (ebook) | ISBN 9781608337439 (e-book) | ISBN 9781626982772 (pbk.)

Subjects: LCSH: Church work with people with social disabilities. | Church work with the poor—Catholic Church. | Marginality, Social—Religious aspects—Catholic Church. | Mission of the church. | Catholic Church—Doctrines. | Francis, Pope, 1936-

Classification: LCC BV4461.8 (ebook) | LCC BV4461.8 .R5313 2018 (print) | DDC

261—dc23

LC record available at https://lccn.loc.gov/2017040789

Contents

Introduction: Pope Francis's Proposal   **1**

1. The Return of the Margins   **7**
The Global City and the New Margins   7
Church of the South   12
The Turn Taken by Francis   17
The Church Was at the Center   20
A World That Is Alien to the Church   23

2. The Ancient Margins of Christianity   **31**
Bible and Margins   31
The Galilean Accent   35
The Poor, the Excluded, and the Margins   41
The Statement of the Center   48
A Center That Became Marginal   51
Flight from the World for the Desert   56

3. Some Marginal Fragments of Christian Life   **65**
Descending to the Depths   65

Becoming a Foreigner in Your Own
      Country   70
The Russian Church Seen from Siberia   73
A Nun in the Camp   79
A Twentieth-Century Roman Fool for
      Christ   85

4. **Mission on the Margins**   **95**
The Growth of Contemporary Margins   95
Estrangement from Christianity   99
Paris and a Concerned Cardinal   104
France, a Mission Country?   110
A Brief Big Story   112
About a Failure: So Many Questions   123
A Testing Place for the Centrality of
      Christianity   126
The Mystique of the Margins   132
Women on the Margins   137
A Woman in the Marxist City   142
Sant'Egidio: The Poor Suburbs and the
      City   149

Conclusion: Gospel on the Margins   **163**

Notes   *177*

Introduction

Pope Francis's Proposal

Immediately after his election, Pope Francis called everybody's attention to the subject of "the margins." These are not just the poor suburbs on the outskirts of big cities but areas, situations, and people that are marginal or marginalized in other ways. In Christianity the margins have a long and complex history; indeed, they have been a meeting point of different histories and experiences. Bergoglio revived the church's interest in this subject. That can already be seen in his speech at the cardinals' meeting before the 2013 conclave that elected him pope. The then-archbishop of Buenos Aires said before his election:

> The Church is called upon to come out of itself and go to the margins, not only geographical, but also in human terms, where the mystery of sin, pain, injustice, and ignorance dwells, where there

is contempt for religious and for religious thinking, and where there are all kinds of misery.[1]

That is a succinct but fair expression of the thinking of Jorge Mario Bergoglio. The church must reach out to those areas he calls the margins of society—the world of the marginalized and excluded, all kinds of poor people who live outside the rich world.

Going out to the margins had long been Archbishop Bergoglio's experience in the great city of Buenos Aires. Indeed, in his pastoral work in the Argentine capital we find a theology of the city that is rather rare in contemporary Catholicism, a vision in which the margins—the excluded—play a decisive part. It is a theology closely linked to the lived experience of the church where Bergoglio was archbishop. History, personal experiences, theological reflection, and concerns about the future come together in the mature vision of the Argentine pope.

In his first speech at the conclave we find two themes that recur during Francis's papacy: the need for the church to go outward and, at the same time, to go out to the geographical and existential margins. This is a direction he proposes for twenty-first century Christians in his programmatic text, the apostolic exhortation *Evangelii Gaudium*. In it the pope invites us to "go forth from our own comfort zone in order to reach all the 'peripheries' in need of the light of the Gospel" (no. 20). Indeed, this is a baseline for Pope Francis's whole papacy.

That feeling also marked the geography of his pastoral journeys; Francis started from the margins to get to the center. He also did this in Italy, the country in which, as pope, he serves as primate. First, he visited Lampedusa, the island where the migrants and refugees were landing, then certain minor dioceses, not arriving for the first time in a big city until two years after his election, with his visit to Naples. He did the same in the rest of Europe. In 2016 he had not yet visited the capital cities where Catholicism is an important reality with great historical significance, such as Paris, or Madrid, but he had been to Albania and Sarajevo. He went to Ireland, which, since the clerical sex-abuse scandal, has become a "margin" in the Catholic world. In Latin America he went to Brazil for World Youth Day, a trip that had already been planned by Benedict XVI, but then, in 2015, he chose to enter the continent via a detour through Ecuador, Bolivia, and Paraguay, countries which by and large are marginal. Later in the same year he also visited Cuba on his way to the United States. In 2016 he went to Mexico, a country which John Paul II visited at the beginning of his papacy.

The margins are a special place for Christian presence. First and foremost, the church and its activity address the marginalized, the poor, and the excluded. This is not just a "charity" option but a specific historical-geographical option rooted in the history of Christianity. Francis has grasped this: Christianity must be reborn from the marginal and excluded worlds and thence reach or return to the center. The pope, who comes from the megalopolis of Buenos Aires (with nearly three million inhabitants and thirteen million in its metropolitan area), knows how much of its social and religious life is lived on the margins. It is an illusion to concentrate everything on the center or regard the center as a city's dominant reality. Of course, in the marginalized areas the church's presence is weaker than its institutionalized structures in the historical centers or in districts with a solid pastoral history. In Bergoglio's vision it is not just an ecclesiastical, pastoral, or organizational question but the conviction—as we have said—that in today's world so much takes place on the margins and these marginalized worlds should be brought back into the heart of the church.

Besides that conviction, there is another which is far from secondary: Christianity should make a "preferential option" for the excluded and marginalized. This springs from the gospel: the church's so-called "option for the poor" is its true historical and geographical task.[2] We could call it "Pope Bergoglio's Gospel Geopolitics" or simply *geotheology*. This is not something impromptu or pragmatic; it comes from lived conviction and the depth of the church. Vatican II reinvigorated it by raising the subject of the church of the poor. Of course the poor and the marginalized overlap and are the same people, but we should note that the use of the geographical expression *marginal* has a particular connotation in the pope's language.

With this in view, Pope Francis decisively invited Christians to confront the world's excluded, which means starting again from the poorest and where they live. However, though the marginalized have been important in Christian history, it goes without saying that the reality and significance of the marginal worlds have changed very rapidly, especially in recent years. In the marginalized exclusion zones, we see, as if in a seismograph, the course of history and the earthquakes that shake the social lives of millions of people. These marginalized areas are changing quickly. What are they like today? What does it mean to return to them, as Pope Francis proposes?

As we shall see, the call to go to the margins has roots in the earliest history of the church. In subsequent centuries, as the Catholic Church increasingly identified itself with the "center," that call to the margins has resurfaced in many forms—often in ways that sought to renew the gospel message or to rescue its credibility and relevance. Sometimes, as with the rise of monasticism, the mendicant movements of the Middle Ages, or apostolic communities in the modern era, these initiatives had broad social influence. In other cases, such as the French worker priests in the mid-twentieth century, they were suppressed. In still other cases, they represented no more than a prophetic witness. In any case, the memory of these various experiments is an important resource as we contemplate the world of the margins in our own time, and consider the meaning and implication of Pope Francis's call.

1

The Return of the Margins

The Global City and the New Margins

With increasing globalization the subject of the margins is the order of the day in the debate on the city and how different social groups live together in the new scenarios created by global urbanization. The classic model of the European city, in which the central square is the meeting place and heart of city life, is now in crisis and under attack from the growth of the marginal zones and urban expansion. It has been an important model, admired and reproduced in many latitudes; but today it has often become a relic of the past. Even in Europe, historical cities have expanded by building outer rings of districts that are increasingly marginalized. These have changed the social reality of the city and created communication difficulties. In short, there is a stratification of the margins and a transformation of the city, even where the classic model has survived.

The growth of these new cities, especially in the global South, where most of the megalopolises are, has given rise to very different urban models. In São Paulo, Brazil, the historic center, with its cathedral square and old economic-financial center, has become sidelined in the city's development of luxury districts and multiple outskirts on the margins. They are all now part of an enormous metropolitan area.

We have also seen the transformation of the old European cities; the historic center, with its network of streets and squares, has progressively emptied. This is the case with Rome, though it has still has not become a megalopolis, as many other world cities have. Its center, the historic city, so rich in monuments (where until just over half a century ago rich and poor coexisted side by side with the presence of so many institutions), has become a container of bureaucratic activities, a market, and shop window for tourists. This has caused a centrifugal displacement to the margins, which have lost any connection with the center or have a weakening relation to it. In this marginalization process the city's common identity and the common lot of its population are getting lost.

The experience of Paris has been different. It has a large historic center, which still fulfills various functions, including residential. Nevertheless, Paris is surrounded by an enormous periphery, the so-called *banlieue,* which represents a world apart and has also absorbed traditional rural centers. It was in the context of this urban reality that the youth revolt of the *banlieues* took place between 2005 and 2006. That demonstrated their low level of social integration, especially for those of non-French origin.

What has happened in French society, which until recently had a great capacity for social integration? According to Jean Daniel, an acute observer of national affairs for more than half a century, "All the social integration mechanisms have gone awry. Army gone. Church less strong. Weaker trade unions. Schools in trouble. As well as all this, there have been massive waves of migrants from black Africa and the Magreb, who could not be integrated as happened in the past."[1] In these poor suburbs the mechanisms for social integration and even social life go awry and not just in France. The harsh reality of the huge Paris *banlieue* area drew general attention because a certain number of "foreign fighters" and terrorists grew up in these environments. Are the margins places that foster revolt?

Those who live on the margins are often lonely, with a sharp reduction in community and family ties (political parties, trade unions, religious communities, associations, and so forth). Where there is no community, social integration becomes difficult. In fact, it is the community that fosters social integration. The social problems of many European countries today lie on the margins. Government policy cannot ignore this reality, also for security reasons. The margins are a challenge to the whole society and an emergency for national politics.

In the face of these anonymous marginal areas—as we also see in so many cities in the global South—the better-off citizens react by constructing defensive areas, controlled and guarded compounds, or gated communities. That is how they protect themselves from the uncertainty of urban living, crime, and mafia networks. After the end of the Cold War, Hans Magnus Enzensberger stressed that the problem of so many cities was "molecular violence," especially in the South: "For some time now civil war has entered the metropolises. Its metastases are an integral part of the daily life of big cities: Mass organized criminality has become a phenomenon that goes beyond traditional standards; it is a new war. We see it, for example, today in Mexico."[2] But it can also be observed among the youth of Central America, in particular with the *maras,* youth mafias that dominate whole areas of El Salvador and Honduras. Enzensberger notes:

All those who don't just leave barricade themselves. At the international level everywhere people are reinforcing the *limes* built to defend themselves from the barbarians. For some time now in

American, African and Asian megalopolises there
have been bunkers for the privileged, surrounded
by impregnable walls and protected by barbed
wire. Sometimes there are whole districts which
cannot be entered without a special pass card.
Electronic barriers, television cameras and well
trained dogs control access . . . the privileged pay
for the luxury of their total isolation.[3]

Wherever they live, anyone outside these protected
compounds is marginalized from the world that counts.
Frequently, the historic centers become marginalized
from the focal points of the city's life. In many cases the
margins mean insecurity. Anyone visiting Johannesburg
becomes aware of many protected compounds or closed
off and guarded market quarters linked by great mo-
torways. The marginalized live outside the city or in its
rundown center. Thus cities are deeply divided between
first-class citizens and the marginalized. As Manuel Castells notes, the first-class citizens are networked with the
global community and have interests reaching far beyond
their own city. Perhaps they are isolated in special areas
or environments from their fellow citizens in the life
of the city, but they are people belonging to the global
world. On the other hand, the Catalan scholar continues, the marginalized citizens live in a geographically
and socially marginal world: "two separate, segregated

life-worlds."[4] The city becomes less and less a community with a common life and lot. Indeed, the city becomes an immense urban backdrop and less and less a community with its own history. As well as this, the new large urban centers absorb the countryside, with its own settlements and functions, creating a very different relationship between city and country from that which has been the case for centuries.

Zygmunt Bauman is one of the scholars who has reflected most on the repercussions of the global world on the life of the city and its inhabitants. He too notes that the sense of the city as a community with a common lot has gone. The marginalized world does not participate, or participates less and less, in the identity and common fate of the urban community. At most, it represents just these marginal, sometimes closed, communities. In fact, Bauman concludes bitterly, "Cities have become dumping grounds for the problems caused by globalization."[5] The margins are the place where the problems of globalization fall heaviest: the true "dumping grounds" for social and human problems.

Church of the South

Between the nineteenth and twentieth centuries Christianity developed from North to South. For the Catholic

Church, growth came through the work of missionaries, men and women who came mostly from European countries and generously went to live in the global South. The Roman Congregation for the Evangelization of Peoples (more widely known by its former name, the Sacred Congregation for the Propagation of the Faith), by which the Holy See pushed forward and carried out this missionary task, largely took over control of this activity from the "Catholic powers" that had promoted not only the conquest of America, but also its evangelization. The Propagation of the Faith model was government from Rome—from the North—of missionary activity and the churches in the South by supporting and channeling human and material energies.

Between the two world wars, with Pius XI, independent dioceses in the South began to be created. That started in China, home to an important ancient civilization. After the Second World War and with decolonization, the drive to set up independent dioceses became unstoppable. That meant creating an episcopal center in marginal lands. But the problem was not that, or not only that. It was a matter of becoming aware—not in ethnic or nationalistic terms—of a church belonging more and more to the global South. For, in fact, the model of church government was still—at least partly—directed from North to South.

In 1974 missiologist Walter Bühlmann proposed a new reading of the Catholic world in a book with the significant title: *The Coming of the Third Church*. He writes:

> The Third Church is not something fallen from the sky. It comes as the end product of a historical process, of what we call the history of the missions, of a centrifugal movement, of a certain migration of people within the Church. It is all part of the mystery of the Church.[6]

According to Bühlmann, it was necessary to accept the fact that the church had become universal, as never before in its two-thousand-year-old history, through the growth—not just numerical—of churches in what was then called the Third World. The churches on the margins now loomed strongly upon the horizon of Catholicism. This phenomenon did not take place only among Catholics but also in the Anglican and evangelical worlds. The Orthodox churches remained outside this growth in Christianity in the global South, because they were substantially located in the European East or in the Middle East (or their diaspora).

During the 1970s a position like Bühlmann's seemed too advanced, even though he captured a situation that was actually occurring. He was not exempt from attacks, even unfair ones. It was still difficult in Catholicism to grasp the reality in a process of rapid change. Recognizing these new dimensions of Catholicism does not mean subscribing to a myth of the churches of the South as if they were a messianic people in relation to the churches of the North. Nevertheless, this reality of third-world Christianity—which arose on the margins—became objectively relevant at the universal level with its own history and profile. When Bühlmann spoke of a third church, he was alluding to the churches of Latin America, Africa, and Asia.

This was not just about the end of mission, as it had previously been conceived, but an attempt to establish a new global mission for Christianity, in both the South and the North. Hence, during his visit to Uganda, which was the first time a pope had visited Africa, Paul VI suggested to the Africans that they themselves should become missionaries in their own countries.[7] Today the vision of a planetary Christianity is here. It is thought that the Catholics in Latin America represent a good 42 percent of the faithful in the world. Missionaries coming from the North are generally fewer, and now nearly all dioceses are independent, each with its own profile and personality within the universal Catholic Church.

Writing about twenty-first century Christianity the American historian of religions Philip Jenkins also speaks of a third church to stress how global Christianity increasingly features the South. (In fact, this is true not only for Catholic but also for Protestant and neo-Protestant Christianity):

> To take one aspect of these startling rediscoveries, consider Christianity's deep association with poverty. Contrary to myth, the typical Christian is not a white fat cat in the United States or western Europe, but rather a poor person, often unimaginably poor by Western standards
>
> The grim fact of Christian impoverishment becomes all the more true as Africa assumes its place as the religion's principal center.[8]

The Christianity of the South is not only characterized by geographical dislocation, but also by the marginal status of its adherents, because they live on the margins. Think of the megalopolises of the world's South. Jenkins observes that "Christianity is flourishing wonderfully among the poor and persecuted, while it atrophies among the rich and secure."[9] In short, between the twentieth and twenty-first centuries there has been a transformation of Christianity, which is becoming more and more a religion of the margins and the marginalized. This fact is not immediately apparent because we are still tied to old and consolidated ideas of Christianity. But we need to become aware of the reality and the routes taken by this religion to the margins, which are themselves so different from one another and produce different religious experiences and practices. At any rate, the twenty-first-century church has certainly become more of a reality on the margins and is made up of more poor people. And it goes without saying that these margins, even if they are not well integrated into Christianity's official traditional structures, are not without their own religious life; they have their own Christian life, even when it is of their own particular kind.

The Turn Taken by Francis

As archbishop of Buenos Aires, Pope Francis comes from the South. Argentina geographically belongs to the South, but it is also connected to Europe by the origin of much of its population and the stamp this has put upon the culture and character of Argentine people. When he spoke of the margins, Francis raised a question that was already present in Christian debate, and not just recently. The question has deep roots in Christianity itself, which has by no means been unaware in its history of the theme of center and margins or city and margins. But Francis raised a very topical question for the life of Christian communities. Their setting or their relationship with the global margins are a challenge for the future of the church and also for human coexistence.

In fact, this theme had been obscured even in this global era (and perhaps even beforehand) through the choices prioritized by the Christian world, which had largely forgotten the reality of the marginal world. Many communities, institutions, and Catholic personalities concentrated more on recognizing social and ethical values and on guiding public morality, with strong use of the media and engagement in cultural battles. By influencing the center (not just the social but also the political and media center), they believed they were determining social customs in a more relevant way. This position corresponded to the idea that in the global world minorities had to conduct public cultural battles. That appeared to be the task of Catholicism, both in traditional Catholic countries and elsewhere. It was an imprecise interpretation of Benedict XVI's talk of "creative minorities," which stressed how the holiness and creativity of small communities had permeated and molded whole peoples.

Of course, the church's position as a minority defending nonnegotiable values (as it claimed) did not mean leaving its territory unguarded, but it focused attention on the real and virtual center of society. It is true that there has been no lack of Christians in the marginal worlds. But the church's position was a restructuring of Catholicism as a cohesive ethical minority in an extremely pluralistic and relativistic society that radically challenged it. That caused a configuration of Catholicism which had a different task from its historical one, even though it still exalted its traditional aspects.

For Francis the position of embattled minority makes the church lose much of its power of attraction. The speech he gave to the US bishops (leaders of a church that has conducted important public battles on nonnegotiable values) expresses his vision very well:

> Harsh and divisive language does not befit the tongue of a pastor, it has no place in his heart; although it may momentarily seem to win the day, only the enduring allure of goodness and love remains truly convincing.[10]

Pope Francis does not believe in the church's hegemony over society but in the convincing attraction of goodness and love as they are reflected in the life of the church. To his way of thinking, the success of such hegemonies is weak and merely apparent. So the pope invites bishops and Christians to insist upon the attraction of the gospel and of mercy rather than on battles about values.

In his interview with Antonio Spadaro on "Catholic Civilization" Francis maintained:

> "We cannot insist only on issues related to abortion, gay marriage and the use of contraceptive methods. This is not possible. I have not spoken

much about these things, and I was reprimanded for that. But when we speak about these issues, we have to talk about them in a context."[11]

The pope wants to bring the church into contact with human reality, even in its most painful and problematic aspects. By that reality, he means the environments where contemporary women and men live, the world of the great margins, spaces of exclusion and solitude. That seems to be the message of *Evangelii Gaudium,* the manifesto of Bergoglio's papacy.

The Church Was at the Center

It is true that the church was at the center of the city in ancient European societies. That was the result of a long history, and it can be seen in most of the city centers of the prevalent Christian tradition. We see this with the buildings, such as cathedrals, in a central position in most cities with a Christian tradition, or the bishop's palace at the heart of the city that gives the diocese its name. The Duomo in the heart of Milan, actually in the central square, is characteristic of such cities. Even though—as Cardinal Carlo Maria Martini always recalled—in Rome itself the cathedral is not in the center but in what was the margin or outskirts of the Roman city, with the building by Constantine of the Lateran basilica, the Urbe cathedral.[12] That happened because at the time the central positions were occupied by pagan temples. Later it was the great religious orders, like the Jesuits, who built imposing churches in the city center. But apart from Rome, the church is normally set in a central city position.

That position gives it an urbanistic point of view and reflects the centrality of the church in Christian societies after what has been called the Constantinian turning point. The cathedral at the city center expresses the dominant force of the church's presence as the regulator of social life. The Christian regime profoundly marked society and the European city for centuries. The church thought of itself as "the queen of society," the religious and ethical fulcrum of its life, baptizing it with the church's authority and vision. For many centuries the church was at the center of an officially Christian society.

The end of the church's centrality, with the French Revolution, had so many social and religious effects that they cannot even be summarized here. The break was radical. It also caused the "secularization" of Notre Dame Cathedral, which after being devastated, was proclaimed a temple of the Goddess of Reason. With the revolution Catholicism was eliminated from the center of Paris. When the revolutionary period was over, the Restoration tried to reinstate the centrality of Christian buildings and values in society. At the same time it worked, by means of missions, to reconquer the regions most secularized by the revolutionary process. But the time for a wholly Catholic society was over, despite the religious and political efforts to bring it back. A period began in which Christianity was driven, not always successfully or drastically, to the margins of society.

After the French Revolution, during the nineteenth and twentieth centuries, the restoration of the church's central position in public and social life remained a long-term strategic objective for Catholicism. It took many different forms, but the aim was the restoration of a Christian society. This persisted as the church's strategy throughout those centuries. According to church authorities the cathedral could not just stand at the city center like the ancient noble palaces, which were no longer part of public life but still remained there as relics of the past.

Restoration meant really and officially restoring the church to its central position in the city, civil society, in the "heart" of the people, as a purveyor of values, and as a moral teacher in the public sphere. This long-term pastoral and cultural strategy was the driving force of many actions, battles, and campaigns to reconquer the center of the city and, above all, social life. Restoration was a rebellion against the marginalization of the church, of the faith, and of Christian customs in society. Its aim was to regain that position which Christianity traditionally held as its due. However, the restoration of a Catholic society never happened in a satisfactory way, despite all the efforts to promote it in so-called Christian Europe and its cities. In country districts the model of a Christian society survived longer.

Secularization advanced in the twentieth century both among the middle and working classes. A Catholic restoration seemed to become impossible. Major sectors of society consistently distanced themselves from the faith and practice of Christianity. This became widespread social custom. The church, which had been at the center of society for centuries, was unable to regain its former position. Sidelined in the city and in public opinion, it was also beginning to lose its hold on the marginal areas. In the face of this additional crisis, the church relaunched its presence in these marginal sectors with a strategy of conquest from the center. In this way it tried to win over the margins, believing that the center was the creator of models of social behavior for all.

A World That Is Alien to the Church

During the nineteenth and twentieth centuries, while a large part of Catholicism was struggling for restoration, one dramatic occurrence seen in Christianity was the break between the church and the marginal worlds— both city margins and the more marginalized groups in industrial society, such as the urban working-class proletariat. This occurred in a particular way in societies that were industrialized or in the process of industrialization.

In 1877 in France, Claude-Anthime Corbon, an important person who publicly called himself a worker-senator, addressed an open letter to Monseigneur Dupanloup, a widely known French bishop of liberal Catholic tendencies. This bishop's interpretation had helped soften some of the rigid aspects of Pius IX's *Syllabus of Errors,* making it acceptable to part of French public opinion. Corbon's text had this title: *Why We Abandon You.* It was a public reply to a public question asked by Bishop Dupanloup: "Who will tell me why these people abandon us?"

The question expressed a concern spreading among many French Catholics, and not only French ones, about changes happening in society and, in particular, the tumultuous growth of a proletariat often remote from the church. France, England, Belgium, and Germany had already had an industrial revolution, entailing urbanization and the growth of city margins. There had been an exodus from rural areas and a growing proletariat of factory workers and masses of poor people. This was a new people, suffering economic difficulties and hard lives, often far from the practice of religions and traditional Christian faith.

Corbon lived in Paris, a great capital city where an industrial proletariat had arisen. These were the protagonists during the revolution of 1848 and the Paris Commune of 1871, the first communist revolution in history. The Paris Commune, in particular, had been marked by anticlerical features, to the point where the archbishop of Paris, Monseigneur Darboy, had been shot. That had revealed the feelings of many people in Paris. Anticlericalism was strong.

Did the church side with the "powers" in French society? This was the widespread belief among that sector of the working class who put hope for its own betterment in socialism or communism. Senator Corbon replied solemnly to the question asked by Bishop Dupanloup:

> Monseigneur, we abandon you today because for centuries you have abandoned us. When I say that you have abandoned us, I don't mean that you have refused us the "comforts of religion"; no, in your clerical lack of concern you were lavish with these. I mean that for centuries you have abandoned our concerns for this life. Rather, you exercised your influence to prevent our social liberation.[13]

The church had sided with the "masters," so Corbon added: "Your hatred for the Revolution has extinguished love for God."[14] Corbon's reply was harsh, accusing the church of having chosen economic and political power over the interests of the people. In the eyes of the church his reply was unfair; even in Paris, on the margins, there was a significant Catholic presence. But paradoxically, he was telling the truth; the church had not chosen these marginalized people.

Corbon became a senator during the Third Republic. He had been a socialist and utopian Christian in 1848, when he had dreamed of a great social change that would also involve a renewed Christianity. That year had been the "magic year" of revolutions, not only in France but in Europe. Corbon and others had hoped for a meeting and alliance between Catholicism and the working masses, between Catholicism and democracy. In the atmosphere of 1848 that seemed possible. But as the years passed, Corbon began to believe that there had been a divorce between the church and the working-class world. He no longer believed that the church would side with working people and lead them to salvation. He had abandoned that dream, henceforth regarding the church as completely on the side of the economic power and the social and political forces of Restoration.

In his book *Le secret du peuple de Paris [The secret of the people of Paris],*[15] Corbon confirmed his break from the church and proposed the self-liberating autonomy of the people, whose liberation would not come from outside, from the church, but from themselves, from the self-organization of the working class. Nothing further could be expected from the church. Besides, the idea of workers' self-liberation had been developed for more than a century in the socialist and communist movement. The debate between Dupanloup and Corbon emblematically illustrates the drama of the divorce between the church and the working-class world, now a true margin of the city and society. This problem, still unresolved, carried over from the nineteenth to the twentieth century.

This divorce between the church and the working class has worried Catholics and bishops for a long time, especially in Europe. That is well expressed in Pius XI's famous statement that separation represented the greatest scandal of the century. The situation concerned not only France. With industrialization, the displacement of the rural masses toward the cities and their urbanization on city margins became a European phenomenon over a long period. Though Rome was not an industrial city, in the middle of the twentieth century the practice of religion was seen to be very low in its proletarian areas in contrast to its bourgeois districts. The divorce of the poor, the proletariat, the workers was regarded as a laceration of the church throughout the nineteenth and twentieth centuries. The church's response wavered between the priority of a Catholic restoration (in all its different expressions and forms) and that of mission, with redeployment to the marginalized world.

By raising the subject of the margins, Pope Francis today is taking on an issue that has been problematic over a long period. He is following up the central concern of the Second Vatican Council: preaching the gospel to contemporary men and women by sharing their experience of the world and by empathy with their lives. The pope is certainly aware of ethical problems, but he declares the primary importance of going out to the margins and communicating the gospel. Father Jerónimo Nadal (1507–80) wrote about the Society's origins: "We [Jesuits] are not monks. The world is our cloister. The world in our house."[16] And he added a significant expression: "As we are the last and the least . . . we seek what has been abandoned and that is why Father Ignatius set up the missions."[17]

The theme of the marginalized is not a charitable aspect of the church's message but a fundamental repositioning of the human geography of our time. In short, it is something much more vital and strategic than a mere effusion of charitable "kindness." Rather, it is a real and proper restructuring of Catholicism by reconnecting it with the marginal world. The subject of the margins and marginalized is much more fundamental to Christianity than has been thought or said. A strongly doctrinal—or

ideological—reading has often obscured the centrality of this issue, which nevertheless is strongly present
throughout the history and geography of Christianity.
There is a vital link between the margins and marginalized and Christianity itself.

2

The Ancient Margins
of Christianity

Bible and Margins

Margins have a decisive importance in the Bible. Biblical
scholar Ambrogio Spreafico writes that In its long history the land of Israel is "a great margin because it never
became a dominant power of that geographical area but
was nearly always dependent on the countries that suc-
cessively arose around it."[1] The dominant powers were
Egypt, the land of the pharaohs, and the Mesopotamian
area between the two great rivers, the Tigris and the
Euphrates. The land of Israel is really a corridor, a place
of meeting and collision, where all kinds of ruling powers have taken over. The Jews are on the margins of the
great political systems. However, they hold together in
their faith in the one and only God, who enables them—
among other things—not to lose their identity through-

out a troubled history and under political and cultural pressure from the great powers: "a margin within a great world," as Spreafico defines the land of Israel.

The Bible shows how it is faith in the one and only God that guarantees the survival of a people destined by its geographical position to undergo invasions and assimilation. The center was not a land but a God of people who listened to him and opted for him. The faith of Israel was the faith of a marginal land that historically became a center of innovation and change. As we read in the book of Deuteronomy, the Lord declares why he has chosen such a marginal people as his own:

> It was not because you were more numerous than any other people that the Lord set his heart on you and chose you—for you were the fewest of all peoples. It was because the Lord loved you and kept the oath that he swore to your ancestors. (Deut 7:7–8)

God wanted to save his people from slavery, precisely when they were in an extremely marginalized position in the vast Egyptian empire: "The Lord has brought you out with a mighty hand, and redeemed you from the house of slavery, from the hand of Pharaoh king of Egypt" (Deut 7:8). Indeed, the exodus from Egypt has become a model that reaches beyond the history of Israel, and from time to time it has inspired the language of liberation for many other peoples and marginalized communities. A marginal and enslaved people passes through the desert and, after a long journey, finally finds the land and freedom it has been promised. The desert becomes a school for Israel, as Maimonides says in his *Guide for the Perplexed:* God "makes [the people] wander perplexed in the desert until their souls become brave . . . and until young people are born who are not accustomed to humiliation and slavery."[2]

The exodus from the marginalization of slavery in Egypt does not mean immediate arrival in the land of liberation. For this marginal people there is still another marginal world to cross, the test of the desert. However, although it is small and outside the great history of empires, Israel is not forgotten in the desert, just as it was not forgotten in its time of slavery. Rather, God gives the people the commandments and a highly-structured law. The decisive factor is that a marginal people should have relevance and a unique value in God's eyes, even though it is disregarded and trampled on by strong and powerful kingdoms. Israel does not lose its connection with the Lord, despite its sins and errors. Spreafico writes:

> God chooses a marginal people, so that starting from it the history of humanity can be reconstructed. A new history starts from the margins.

God intervenes from the margins to retake his place in the history of the world.[3]

If we may generalize, the biblical writings that have come down to us reach their peak and develop when Israel is in difficult conditions—unfree, marginalized, trampled on by its neighbors—in short, reduced to a marginal people in the international life of its time. In a way the Bible is a marginal history of a marginalized people, who become God's chosen instrument to remake the history of the world. Often when Israel enters the larger history of the time, it is in a marginal state, in exile or slavery. The larger history of the nations that count and their sovereigns is read by the prophets—in contradiction to the current vision—as events that develop around a small people loved by God.

It is the great prophetic theme of Jerusalem, a city so often humiliated and destroyed, that becomes a light for all nations. This is a great vision of hope, while the eyes of the Jews are fixed on the sad reality of the present, where they are marginalized in history. The Jews are called upon to trust in God, who speaks of a different future and declares he has not forgotten them, even though they are in a truly marginalized condition.

The Bible puts us in contact with the great historical visions of hope, communicated and nourished by a marginal people. Are these just consoling utopias of the marginalized? They console but they also show the historical strength of consoling the marginalized. Indeed, as in past centuries, today these visions still nourish the hope and faith of many believers, both Jews and Christians. They are the visions of a marginalized people who believed that salvation could only come from God. And God required them not to count on their powerful neighbors and not to conform to the customs and visions of nations that had a much more salient part in history. At the end of the book of Isaiah we read:

> the glory of the Lord has risen upon
>> you.
> For darkness shall cover the earth
>> and thick darkness the peoples;
> the Lord will rise upon you,
>> and his glory will appear over you.
> Nations shall come to your light,
>> and kings to the brightness of your
>>> rising. (Isa 60:1–3)

The Galilean Accent

During the story of the passion of Jesus we read that Peter was sitting in the high priest's court. People come up to him and say: "Certainly you are also one of them, for your accent betrays you." In self-defense Peter begins to swear: "I do not know the man!" (Matt 26:73–74). It is significant that he is recognized as a disciple of Jesus by his Galilean accent. An accent is not just a leftover from a past history, but distinguishes a person, perhaps forever. An accent shows the trace of the environment from which the person comes. People do not wholly abandon that accent, even when they live far away. An accent denotes what the Germans call *Heimat* (home), one's native land and family. Peter had a Galilean accent, therefore he was a provincial and a man of the margins.

The apostles were Galileans, and so was Jesus. As the Waldensian pastor Valdo Vinay noted acutely a few years ago, Galilee was not only a place of passage and a cross-roads, but in Jesus's time it was also on the margins of Israel, which itself was marginal and under Roman rule.[4] The land of Galilee had its own political and economic peculiarities and was also a mixture of many ethnic components; there was the Jewish Galilee, the Hellenistic Galilee, as well as various other ethnicities. In short, it was a peculiar place as well as being marginal. Certainly it was not homogenous.

So Jesus's message comes from a marginal world. He himself is marked by its accent, as are his best friends. If, as Jesus says, salvation comes from the Jews, the salvation of the gospel comes from a marginal region of the Jewish world. After the arrest of Jesus in Jerusalem, Peter is recognized by his regional accent. The first disciples, who had gone up to Israel's capital city together with their master, were all marginal.

In the gospels marginal Galilee becomes a center for Jesus's preaching. That is where his public ministry opens. The Galilean teacher travels all over his region of Galilee, from one end to the other, like an itinerant prophet, a man without fixed abode, coming close to the people who live there, and knowing their weakness as sheep without a shepherd (Matt 9:36). Until the end of his life, even in its final moments, he remains very attentive to those who are marginalized and excluded. In the Gospels of Matthew and Mark the central plot of the story—the proclamation of the gospel by Jesus— begins at the margins. Luke's plan is different and more extended: Jesus's mission, and that of his disciples after him, moves from Galilee, arrives in Jerusalem, and travels the world until it reaches Rome, the capital of the empire, as we see in the Acts of the Apostles. However, despite their different viewpoints, in all three Gospels the starting point is Galilee, a marginal area that was too "mixed," according to the Jews, who were bent on keeping their identity pure. Furthermore, there was prejudice against the small Galilean town of Nazareth, from which Jesus came. It was an unimportant little place. When Philip the apostle told Nathanael that he had found the one spoken of by Moses and the prophets, Nathanael exclaimed sarcastically: "Can anything good come out

of Nazareth?" (John 1:45–46). Can anything good come
from a small town like Nazareth and a marginal place
like Galilee? In the Gospel that is a significant question.

As the great scholar John P. Meier says, Jesus was
a "marginal Jew"—the title of his book.[5] Perhaps we
could say that Jesus was a marginal man, as is his gospel,
in comparison with Rome, the world-city. He bears the
stamp of the Jewish margins in which he took his first
steps. However, Galilee remains crucial for the new
community, despite the fact that Jesus had gone up to
Jerusalem with his disciples and spent his last dramatic
days there before his death. In Mark's Gospel the first
appointment, conveyed through an angel to the women
who had gathered at the Lord's grave, was in Galilee:
"Go, tell his disciples and Peter that he is going ahead
of you to Galilee; there you will see him just as he told
you" (Mark 16:7). The same announcement is given to
the women in Matthew's Gospel: "Go quickly and tell his
disciples, 'He has been raised from the dead,' and indeed
he is going ahead of you to Galilee; there you will see
him" (Matt 28:7). Jesus goes ahead of his disciples to
Galilee, the place where their relationship began.

In Luke's Gospel all the appearances of the risen Lord
are set in Jerusalem. However, in John's Gospel quite a
lot of space is given to Jesus's meeting with some of his
disciples, including Peter and John, by Lake Tiberias in
Galilee. Thus John's Gospel agrees with Matthew and

Mark on the importance of this marginal region, where his ministry began with the calling of the disciples and the wedding at Cana.

Jesus's message is deeply imbued with the marginal accent of Galilee. The community gathered around him always bears the stamp of Galilee. The region remains very important for the disciples, even after Jesus's death. The risen Jesus is to be met—at least according to Mark, Matthew, and John—in marginal Galilee. What happened in the history of Israel is repeated in the new messianic people, though of course in very different ways. God enters the history of nations through a message that comes from the margins, heard and delivered first by marginal people with Galilean accents. In the story of Jesus of Nazareth God himself becomes marginalized to the point where someone asks whether anything good can come out of Nazareth.

The Gospel starts from the margins and goes out to embrace Israel and the world. That is the plan of Luke's story, which starts from Galilee, then goes up to Jerusalem, the place of Jesus's death and resurrection. It continues with the Gospel's first journey outside Israel, through the preaching of the apostles and Paul, related in the Acts of the Apostles. They leave the margins—in this case Jerusalem, where the apostles are gathered for Pentecost—and follow a complex route ending in Rome. This is also a journey from the margins to the center of the imperial Roman world. Indeed, in Acts the story stops just when the apostle Paul arrives in Rome.

While they are still in Jerusalem after Peter's first preaching at Pentecost, the small community experiences a larger world speaking in different languages and coming from different countries. The description of the people hearing the apostles' words at Pentecost represents the whole world, which will be reached by the gospel. Yet, when Peter and the apostles speak to the people of Jerusalem at Pentecost, the mission to the world is only a dream of marginal Galileans, who are so imbued with the Holy Spirit that they appear drunk. The miracle of Pentecost strengthens the aspiration of these marginal people and the *parresia* (outspokenness) of their preaching as Galileans to a wider world than theirs.

The first-generation church was not ashamed of Peter's accent, even though the force of his preaching was enriched by so many other accents, including that of an exceptional figure like Paul. Paul was a Roman by name and citizenship. He inhabited three worlds and three cultures, Jewish, Greek, and Roman. Like so many of the Jewish elite, he was a polyglot and accustomed to different languages and alphabets. Paul had the genius to translate the gospel message into different languages and cultures. But that first-generation message did not lose contact with its Galilean origins. Peter's martyrdom in Rome shows how a man from the margins, without any international experience, could challenge the harshness and complexity of the capital of the world with the "folly" of his preaching.

When the two figures are set side by side—and remembering the martyrdom of both in Rome—the figure of the Galilean Peter completes that of Paul, the cosmopolitan Jew. The master came from the margins, as did the first of his apostles, Peter, who, according to tradition, died as a martyr in the great capital city of the empire. Jesus had said that salvation comes from the Jews. We could say that the gospel message of salvation comes first of all from the margins, from Galilee and the land of Israel, subject to Roman rule.

The Poor, the Excluded, and the Margins

The Gospels' link to the margins is not that nostalgic tie to *Heimat* (home) but derives from a persistent relationship with people who are marginalized, in whatever village or city Jesus goes to preach his word. Indeed, the idea of the margins is not just political, ethnic, or geographical; the margins are the land of the marginalized, the excluded. However, they are not excluded by God; God has not forgotten them. So the marginalized and the margins accompany the preaching of the gospel by Jesus and his disciples as a permanent reality. The marginalized receive their attention and care and are at the heart of their activities. From Mary's *Magnificat* on, the Gospels resound with the proclamation that God

> has brought down the powerful from
>   their thrones,
>   and lifted up the lowly (Luke 1:52).

That fundamental feature of the gospel message has provoked strong criticisms of the Christian faith as a religion of the poor and defeated, including that of Friedrich Nietzsche:

Christianity has taken the side of everything weak, base, ill-constituted, it has made an ideal out of opposition to the preservative instincts of strong life. . . . That strange and sickly world into which the Gospels lead us—a world apparently out of a Russian novel, in which the scum of society, nervous maladies and "childish" idiocy keep a tryst—must, in any case, have coarsened the type: the first disciples, in particular, must have been forced to translate an existence visible only in symbols and incomprehensibilities into their own crudity, in order to understand it at all.[6]

In fact, Jesus identifies himself with the marginalized. That emerges clearly from the parable of the last judgment:

"I was hungry and you gave me food, I was thirsty and you gave me something to drink, I was a stranger and you welcomed me, I was naked and you gave me clothing, I was sick and you took care of me, I was in prison and you visited me." Then the righteous will answer him, "Lord, when was it that we saw you hungry and gave you food, or thirsty and gave you something to drink? And when was it that we saw you a stranger and welcomed you, or naked and gave you clothing? And when was it that we saw you sick or in prison and visited you?" [that is, when did we ever see you in that marginalized state?] And the king will answer them, "Truly I tell you, just as you did it to one of the least of these who are members of my family, you did it to me." (Matt 25:35–40).

The poor are the marginalized in life. Jesus identifies with them more than with any others. It is an extraordinary fact in the Gospels and deserves attention and is the reason for the permanent link between Christians and the marginalized. The only others with whom he identifies in this way are those persecuted for the sake of the gospel. "Saul, Saul, why are you persecuting me?" The apostle hears the voice of Jesus himself saying this to him on the road to Damascus (Acts 9:4).[7] This is a very clear, realistic declaration of the gospel, which John Chrysostom developed with matchless power in his preaching, as a central theme that was not always so prominent in the fathers of the church. Commenting on the story of the magi in Matthew's Gospel, Chrysostom says:

> If those men journeyed so far to see Him newly born, what sort of excuse will you have, not going out of your way one alley's length, that you may visit Him sick or in bonds? And yet when they are sick or in bonds, even our enemies have our pity; yours is denied even to your Benefactor and Lord. And they offered gold, you hardly give bread. They saw the star and were glad, you, seeing Christ Himself a stranger and naked, are not moved.[8]

Jesus is the one who is sick, in prison, in distress. That is the faith of the church fathers. John Chrysostom stresses this frequently. Commenting on John's Gospel, Chrysostom gives voice to Christ himself:

> Yet still for very nature's sake be softened at seeing Me naked, and remember that nakedness wherewith

I was naked on the Cross for you; or, if not this, yet that wherewith I am now naked through the poor. I was then bound for you, nay, still am so for you, that whether moved by the former ground or the latter, you might be minded to show some pity.[9]

In these words we see very clearly the gospel realism in which Jesus is present in the poor. The poor and the marginalized are Christ himself, the sign of his presence among us:

You eat to excess—says Chrysostom—but Christ does not even eat what is necessary; you have varied dishes, he not even dry bread . . . when he was thirsty you did not even give him a cup of cold water; you sleep on a soft and embroidered bed, but he is perishing with the cold . . . let Christ sit down to eat with you. If he shares your salt and your table, he will be mild in judging you. . . . Don't mind the poor man coming to you filthy and squalid, but consider that Christ through him is setting foot in your house, and stop being unkind, cease your harsh words, with which you reproach those who come to you.[10]

The Orthodox theologian Olivier Clément, a great teacher of humanity and gospel wisdom, speaks of a sacrament of the poor in line with this patristic tradition. That is Chrysostom's theology: the poor person is another Christ. In the poor, Christ himself becomes marginalized, a beggar, a prisoner; he comes to us in the person of the poor and their needs. Jesus lives permanently on the margins and among the poor, and through them he presents himself to Christians. So, in some way, the houses, bodies, and lands of the marginalized are where the teacher from Nazareth still lives. He was born in an outbuilding in Bethlehem, because there was no room for him in the inn. The nativity scene of poverty always reminds us of the poverty of the marginalized.

During Jesus's passion, while the apostles—marginalized Galileans—fled in terror, the Lord's cross was put onto the shoulders of a man who had come from outside Jerusalem, from the country: "They compelled a passerby, who was coming in from the country, to carry his cross; it was Simon of Cyrene, the father of Alexander and Rufus" (Mark 15:21). This marginal man, who comes from the country, has to carry Jesus's cross for part of the way. He is the only one who does. Citizens are not obliged to carry out this onerous and humiliating task. Simon's name must have been well known to Mark's community, so the evangelist gives some details about him and his name remains in the story of the passion.

The poor and the marginalized must have a special position in the lives of Christian believers and the community.

It is necessary to make room for them and listen to them. Ambrose, bishop of Milan, teaches:

> Someone with no clothes to cover himself cries out in front of your house and you despise him; the naked man beseeches and you are worried about what marble you should use for your floor. The poor man asks you for a little money and gets nothing. He begs you for a bit of bread, and your horse is treated better than him. . . . The people are starving, and you close up your barns. . . . You disgraceful man, in whose power it lies to save the lives of so many from death, and you have no will to do so![11]

Throughout history Christians have sometimes pushed the poor in their communities out to the margins, behaving disgracefully, as Ambrose says. The disgrace in the lives of Christians and the church itself arises from their detachment from the poor and their distance from where poor people live. The preaching of the great fathers of the church—Ambrose, Gregory the Great, John Chrysostom—constantly urged putting the marginalized at the center of Christian life and the life of the church; they saw Jesus himself in the poor, who are a sacrament of his presence.

Listening to the poor means turning attentively to the margins of life. For indeed, the margins are not only geographical or on city outskirts, but also a social and human reality. A marginal person is one who is excluded from the center of society, where there is power, wealth and well-being. If we are looking for Jesus, he is to be found among the marginalized and on the margins. That is the gospel message.

The Statement of the Center

Nevertheless, we cannot avoid the feeling that this theology of the marginalized and the margins (as well as the practice inspired by it) has itself remained marginal in the church's life. It is hardly necessary to mention the Constantinian turning point which—in various stages—made Christianity the official religion of the Roman Empire. Rome, the ancient center of the empire, and Constantinople, the "new Rome" that the emperor had built in the East, became the two Christian cities, the sacred centers of Christianity. It could be said that Christianity deeply penetrated these two cities, the one with its long history well before Christianity and the other that arose through the will of the emperor.

The reign of Christendom pursued a type of society in which the solidly Christian center radiated out into the geographical margins. That was the role of Rome,

Christianity's holy city, on the one hand, but on the other, also of New Rome, Constantinople, at least until the Ottoman conquest. Moreover, the myth of Rome survived the decadence of the first Rome and the Muslim conquest of Constantinople, projecting itself into the new Christian capital of Russia, Moscow, the "third Rome." The Christian city par excellence is the reality and symbol of the reign of Christendom, which pervades and dominates social life, regulates its rhythms, guides its customs, and blesses its political power.

Can we speak of marginalized and margins in this long "Christian" history? Of course we cannot say that the marginalized were absent, as we see from the care for the poor, that service the churches delivered with greater or less commitment at different historical periods. There has always been a space for charity and charismatic initiatives in Christian communities. Neither were the margins completely forgotten, as can be seen from waves of missionary preaching and evangelization. These show that the center was not closed off in itself but felt the need to go outward in mission work beyond its own geographical and cultural frontiers. Many examples of this can be recalled, stories of charismatic initiatives of Christian communities and monks and nuns.

Nevertheless, over the long term, there tended to be a divorce between the church and the margins. We could say that space for the margins and the marginalized was often related to the gospel character of different periods in the church's history. From time to time people of faith rediscovered the misery of the poor and brought it back into the heart of the church, taking practical care of those in want, either personally or through various good works. But what consideration did the poor have in spirituality, in the life and theology of the church? Was care for the marginalized just a meritorious work of charity?

To confine ourselves to the last two centuries in Europe, according to Olivier Clément, the real drama was the divorce between the sacrament of the altar and the sacrament of the poor, the poor whose hopes were disappointed or not met. From that divorce arose the explosive socialist movement and a struggle for justice that presented itself as an alternative to Christianity. Thus the sacrament of the Eucharist was abandoned by those who were passionately involved in the sacrament of the poor. The marginalized

> rebelled and looked to hopes and the violence of utopias, the passionate expectation of a "millennial reign" . . . brought about by a liberating catastrophe. . . . It is not a matter of replacing the sacrament of the altar with the sacrament of the poor, as the "progressives" do. That means abandoning history to itself so that it becomes just a *danse macabre*. It is a matter of giving the Eucharist its full ethical weight.[12]

This is not just the history of the last two centuries, which gave rise to socialism as a force for the liberation of the oppressed, but a recurrent reality in the church's long life. The poor have not constantly been a "sacrament" for Christians, as Clément would put it. The marginalized have sometimes been blanked out by the center, which was preeminent and thought of itself as a sacred place and the driving force of Christian life. That also meant the adoption of a "central" culture and vision as well as a "centralistic" view of reality and politics (which also meant conformity). Indeed the center—of any society—organically guaranteed the Christian management of the civil community and its denominational character. That process also meant the blanking out of the living presence of the poor in the life of the church. This happened in different ways but they are all connected. The church's missionary expansion crystallized into an "imperial" practice and vision, a spiritual imperialism, which did not disdain the collaboration of political powers to extend itself over the whole world.

A Center That Became Marginal

On the other hand, at certain times of crisis for the center—think of Rome at the time of Gregory the Great—the margins and the marginalized acquired a decisive role, pointing the way to a future of hope. Under pressure from the barbarians, with Italy undergoing a series of battles and constant instability, Rome became a city in decadence and under threat. Although it preserved its memory of past glory and kept it moral authority, Rome became marginal in relation to the new equilibrium of the empire, which had moved to the East. The Urbe, with its splendid monuments recalling a glorious past, was now marginal in relation to the true capital of the empire, Constantinople, and also in relation to the geo-political interests of the imperial system.

In this politically disturbing situation of insecurity for the Roman church and the survival of the city itself, let alone its citizens, Gregory the Great pointed out a new way. He did not reclaim the greatness of the past or seek to restore it through political action. He did not speak nostalgically about restoration. Despite being a great Ro-man, he accepted, painfully, the situation of the ancient capital and of Italy as a whole. But he pointed to a way forward through preaching and the constant re-offering of the word of God to the people.

A center like Rome will save itself if its people listen to the word of God (and here that means the important role of Pope Gregory as its preacher) and set the Lord at the center of their lives. But Rome will also save itself if it pays attention to the poor. This message is strongly linked to the former one. Gregory the Great speaks powerfully about the central role of the poor in the life of Christians and the church. While a world is coming to an end (the world of Rome, which seemed eternal), the pope points to the way forward with the word of God and through the poor. These are clear signs of a future for the church and the city in a period in which Rome as the great political and ecclesiastical center is falling into decadence. It seems as if the world is ending; in fact, many people thought the fall of Rome was the forewarning of the end of the world. But Pope Gregory pointed to the signs of a new age. These signs show the way to salvation and how to undertake the necessary exodus.

With this non-nostalgic attitude, neither rancorous nor prey to the logic of restoration, Gregory pointed his faithful to the way forward and defined the attitude of the Roman church, which had become marginal in the new order that was arising. New peoples inhabited the Italian peninsula, and the center of the imperial system had moved to the East. In this political period, despite its prestige and its history, Rome is in fact marginal. And so, at least partly, is its church.

Pope Gregory's church, which was not strong in political power, nevertheless exercised remarkable authority over the Christian communities of the Mediterranean through the credibility of its message and its apostolic tradition. Despite all its problems and anxieties, under the leadership of Gregory the Great, the church was by no means closed in upon itself or overwhelmed by the crises and difficulties. Rather, in this difficult time, it not only looked to the marginalized people living in the city (the poor at a time of crisis) but also to the far-off geographical margins, such as Anglia (modern England), where the pope sent missionaries to undertake the work of evangelization.

His letters to Augustine of Canterbury, who led the mission to Anglia, reveal the attention Gregory paid to this far-away world at a time when his city and his church were beset by so many problems. Why bother with the evangelization of the Angles and not just consolidate his own position? Even a church like Pope Gregory's, in grave difficulty because of the political situation and the prevailing insecurity, was not reduced to thinking only of itself and its problems but could project itself toward the margins of the then-known world.

The story of Gregory the Great's church is emblematic; it shows it is not necessary to be at the nerve center of history—where imperial Rome with all its resources had been set—to take care of the margins and especially to maintain its gospel vocation. Even from a now-marginalized city such as Rome (although it still had its great reputation and the special authority of its bishop), a genuine and practical interest could be shown for the margins, even the remotest ones. The story of Gregory the Great's Rome shows how a Christian world that had become marginalized—a marginal community—can become the center of attention, courage, enterprise, and initiatives to spread the gospel to other societies. This is a very important lesson in Christian history. Gregory the Great's church was an authoritative center of apostolic preaching. Even in its political and human humiliation it looked far afield. And this was so not only because of its authority but because of its adherence to the gospel.

Many centuries later, between the twentieth and twenty-first centuries, the church of Constantinople, heir to the important Byzantine tradition (the church supported by the imperial power at the time of Gregory the Great and then the leading Orthodox Church after the break with Rome), has been reduced to a small Greek minority in a Muslim and Turkish city. The ecumenical patriarchate is barely a shadow of what it was during the Byzantine or even the Ottoman eras. The ecumenical patriarchate has become a marginal ecclesiastical institution in the politics of modern Turkey. Its very survival is under threat. Nevertheless, this church has developed important ecumenical initiatives, particularly with the outreach of Patriarch Athenagoras and Patriarch Bartholomew, giving it an unprecedented universal range.

Being on the margins does not mean turning in on oneself in a defensive or nostalgic way. With faith, a great message can come from the margins, both for the center and the whole world.

Flight from the World for the Desert

In the history of Christianity the margins sometimes become eloquent for all Christians. They change the lives of Christians at the center, often creating a tension about their possessions and lifestyle. We cannot fail to recall the complex story of the monastic movements of the East and West. In monasticism the margins have an important role in relation to the Christianity of the city. The monks took refuge in rural areas and the desert, worlds on the margins of cities, often in uninhabited places, to live the gospel in an authentic way. They chose to become marginalized in relation to city life, but also in relation to the city church and the lifestyle pursued there. At the end of the 1960s Harvey Cox rightly invited us to take a look at monasticism beyond the stereotypes: "All in all monasticism was a huge multi-form experiment in alternative styles of community living."[13] For centuries monasticism represented a whole array of Christian lifestyles that set themselves on the social and ecclesial margins.

These monastic movements left an important stamp on Christianity. But monasticism is mainly a story of the margins. The choice to live in marginal worlds was not the only driving force of monastic life. The main motive was faithfulness to the gospel in a state of freedom. But being on the margins and in poverty was a way of guaranteeing the conditions for such Christian freedom.

In a true best seller of monastic life like *The Life of Saint Anthony,* a text that inspired many who followed in his footsteps, we read that the father of monasticism lived alone for many years in the desert. Here the saint found there were already hermits leading lives of prayer and work. Monasticism is a long story that in various forms comes from far away. The desert was a real margin for Anthony in relation to the great city of Alexandria between the third and fourth centuries. After that long experience of prayer and solitude, Anthony met many who wanted to follow him: "And thus it finally happened that cells arose even in the mountains, and the desert was colonized by monks, who abandoned their goods and enrolled themselves in the heavenly city."[14]

The desert, a truly marginal region, was populated by Christians who wanted to follow the gospel away from the temptations and logic of the city. The monk's marginal home became another city, ruled by the gospel, a "heavenly" city as an alternative to the earthly city, separated from it by its marginal character. When he left the desert after years of monastic life, Anthony intervened in the life of the city of Alexandria and its church, but in the end he returned to the marginal space he had chosen as the setting for his Christian life.

It is this flight from the world, also found in the life of the father of Western monasticism, Benedict of Nursia, that was handed down to us by Gregory the Great. In this text we read that after having studied literature, Benedict wanted to change his life and retire to solitary places. Thus, he made his way to a lonely hidden place called Subiaco, about forty miles from Rome. "Nearby flowed fresh clear water, which first gathered and formed lakes and then went on to become a river."[15] Like that of many monastic fathers, the story of Benedict is of fleeing from the world to search for God in solitude in the desert. That choice was also attractive to others and gave rise to a community of disciples.

> In solitude Benedict progressed without any in-struction on the road of virtue and already his fame spread from mouth to mouth. Meanwhile he gathered many in that place for the service of almighty God. And with the help of Jesus Christ, the Lord, he built twelve monasteries, and in each of them he set an abbot and sent twelve monks. . . . Some noble and pious men from the city of Rome began to go to him and entrusted either themselves or their sons to be brought up in the service of almighty God.[16]

On the margins of Rome, Gregory tells us, he undertook to live apart from the constraints of civil and ecclesiasti-cal life in Rome. He lived by himself, devoted to chang-ing his life. This fact—we are still following Gregory's

story—reveals the progressive attraction of the "monastic margins" for city Christians. It is a story that is
repeated in the lives of the great monastic fathers, who
left the city and sought solitude, almost on the model of
liberation from Egypt with the exodus and wandering in
the desert in search of the promised land. First of all, in
their stories, they nearly always meet someone who has
already made this choice. After a period of solitude they
become a focal point, attracting others, and, always on
the margins, a particular Christian community is built
around them. The monastic margins and these marginalized monks progressively exercised an influence on the
city church and the center of Christian and social life.

Benedict's Italy, Gregory tells us, did not have great
deserts as in Egypt, but it had vast country districts, uninhabited areas, lands of shepherd and peasants, whose
lives were marked by insecurity and poverty. It was a
world of poor marginal people, who lived wretchedly.
They did not enjoy the protection of institutions and
were often at the mercy of violent attackers. Often
the monks worked the land, which in the city and its
surroundings was the occupation of a large number of
slaves. That became the monks' work, who, though free
men, engaged in manual labor.

In their lives these monks created a real synthesis
between prayer and work, as described in the greatest
text of Western monasticism, the *Rule of Saint Benedict*.

A twentieth-century monk and scholar of Benedictine monasticism, Benedetto Calati, notes: "The presence of monks in the desert made a considerable difference. They transformed certain desolate valleys into real oases."[17] Paradoxically, the monks with their communities became spiritual and practical reference points for the poor in the area. For they were set in a world of the poor and marginalized, who lived precariously in the Italian countryside.

We should not forget that at its beginnings monasticism, both in East and West, was a spontaneous spiritual movement in the desert and marginal areas. The desert was not a completely empty space, in Egypt or elsewhere, but sparsely populated: "It had always been the refuge for marauders, murderers, wanted men, and all kinds of criminals."[18] Sometimes in the stories of monks strange individuals crop up, whom the monks lived in contact with. This was a different, alternative world, marginal to the city, outside the networks of urban civilization and its customs and ties. It was also a foreign world to the city church and its structures.

To some extent, for the monks, leaving the city meant leaving that church behind, with its structures, ecclesiastical authorities and the lifestyle of the Christian communities. They went to live a simple life based on the gospel among poor people and outside secure institutional frameworks. The desert fathers also fled the control of bishops. As Calati notes:

> The aim of the monastic Church of the desert which flees from the city, also flees from cultic religiosity in favor of popular piety. In fact monasticism arises as a movement of popular piety, against a Church which was slowly becoming more and more distant from the people.[19]

The monks were not opting for a life of learning but—as Calati stresses—a form of popular piety, based on the Bible, accessible to simple folk even in their own language, and to those in need of help. We should not confuse monasticism at its beginnings with the forms it assumed in succeeding centuries. The flight to the desert or lonely places was a gospel choice to live in free and poor environments, without constraints, without ecclesiastical formalism. From the margins and the standpoint of the gospel these early monks were effectively criticizing the city and the church now living under Christendom, which arose after the time of persecution and martyrdom.

> If monasticism "has a love affair" with the desert, it does so to challenge the *polis*, the powerful, the

city. The polis is the temptation to power. By fleeing to the desert, in a strongly visual culture based
on symbol, gesture and liturgy, the monk visibly
expresses the Christian condition of not having a
settled home but going in search of a future one.[20]

Thus the margins have a strategic role for living in a
different way from in the city. Often from the monastic margins a renewal movement arises that returns to
the city and involves the stable, well-structured urban
Christianity. The monks are called to the city and given
positions of responsibility. The margins were chosen by
Christians as the setting for a new monastic and gospel
way of life, and although they do not offer many resources, they are a place of Christian renewal.

The relationship between the monks and the poor
is important. An example was Paolino di Nola, a monk
and bishop in Campana between the fourth and the fifth
centuries. He came from a great family of landowners.
He erected a building in which he set up his monastery
on the second floor, while the first floor was set aside
for the poor. Reflecting on his theology, Domenico Sorrentino writes that Paolino "interprets the role of the
poor on the floor beneath the monastery as a presence
that strengthens the foundations of his house through
the prayers that are raised to the Lord."[21] The human
margins are not foreign to monastic life or the search

for God. Rather, the margins and marginal people are the soil in which Christianity is reborn, freed from the institutional ties of the Christian city after the Constantinian turning point.

3

Some Marginal Fragments of Christian Life

Descending to the Depths

Research into so many stories of Christianity on the human margins is in some ways still at its beginning. However, we are struck with how, in the Orthodox world, monasticism represents the "elsewhere" in relation to the "Christian" city or the church of the city. Certain people also take important steps whose fundamental direction is to live as marginalized in relation to the church and the civil institutions established and consecrated by religion. That is the story of fools for Christ, about whom much has been written, though their story remains puzzling and peculiar to Western minds. There are Christ's fools in Byzantium, certainly many more than those who have been canonized—saints described as *salos*, the foolish, the holy mad. Between Syria and Egypt, the fools appeared in the monasteries, they behaved in strange ways, they were despised by their fellow monks. But then it was discovered that the mad monk was a secret server of God, a saint to be respected, even to venerate. At that point the fools disappeared from the monastery, fleeing from the esteem that was growing around them. They wandered through the world and news was lost of them.

There is another series of holy fools—the monks who, after having led a life of prayer, returned to the city and behaved in disconcerting ways. The life of Simeon Salos, written in the seventh century, and of Andrea Salos, written in the tenth century, show a hidden holiness in apparently contradictory and marginal lives. With the end of opposition between the monastic movement and city Christianity, but above all with the consolidation of Islam and the end of antiquity, these figures of marginalized Christian fools disappear.

However, the Byzantine tradition was carried on by Russian Christianity. The life of Andrea Salos was translated into Russian in the thirteenth century, and his figure appears as an icon. Slavic Christianity became the fertile soil in which these holy fools, marginalized in relation to the church and its institutions, took root. They were strongly nonconformist and played a prophetic role in relation to the customary forms of Christian life. Their attitudes were anti-institutional toward the hierarchies of church and State.

The first fool for Christ known in Russia, a *yurodivy,* was called Isaac. His story was told by a monk, like him, in the Kiev Monastery of the Caves at the end of the eleventh century. He was a rich merchant who became a monk and began leading a strange life, one outside the norms of established behavior. The story of the fools for Christ in Russia, with various characters in various periods, continued until the beginning of the twentieth century. Among them were pilgrims, beggars, tramps. They were the poor in spirit who embodied the paradox of a "crazy" Christian life lived on the margins in relation to society and the ecclesiastical organization. In Slavic spirituality there is a popular veneration for these figures; analogous figures in the West are regarded as dropouts by society.

The Russian church made saints of fools for Christ, who had chosen poverty of spirit and of life, led the life of ascetics, but remained free and capable of criticism, humor, prophecy, and polemic against the ecclesiastical and political powers. Though they were criticized by the hierarchies during their lifetime, these fools were accompanied and protected by the people's devotion. The first fools for Christ were lay people: "The saint who renounces all the appearances of reason and morality is capable of special clear-sightedness, to discover and denounce all kinds of pious hypocrisy, all the 'false' virtues which cover up profound vice."[1]

Elisabeth Behr-Sigel writes:

> Weak and humiliated in their human reason they appeared thus as strong to the people, in the image of God's mysterious Wisdom which, "despised and crucified by the rulers of this world, is the power of God for those who believe"(1 Cor 1:2).[2]

The image of the kenotic Christ, who lowers himself to death and death on a cross is mysteriously but truly reflected in these fools. In the foolishness, in the disorder of their lives—according to the norms regulated by the church and society—God's "foolish love" is manifested. This "folly" finds its clearest and most overwhelming expression in the foolishness of the cross. It is striking how in a society like Russia, in which the imperial State and the Orthodox Church were in concord, where basically everything was regulated in a religiously consecrated, organic framework, Christian men and women became marginalized by choice. They became strange and mad, showing that Christianity is a folly beyond the sacred order of society. Folly joins with poverty, ascesis, and prayer, but also with a nonconformist lifestyle, a marginal position in relation to a society that gives a central role to the church in the organization of life and the city. The fools for Christ express in an extreme way that paradoxical character of Christian life.

In a period of the decline of religious life in Russia, in the seventeenth century, the police and religious authorities began exercising stricter control over these paradoxical manifestations of Christian life. The church no longer canonized these figures, as it had done in former centuries. Nevertheless, *yurodstvo,* foolishness for Christ, remained an undercurrent in Russian spirituality and religious life, constantly emerging with very peculiar expressions and personalities in which it was not always easy to distinguish prophetic life from unsociability. But it remained a constant in this spirituality.

Moreover, not even Peter the Great, with all his severity and the impact of his Westernizing reforms, succeeded in making this phenomenon disappear. Not even with the strictly antireligious order imposed on society in the Soviet period was this tradition of Christian folly eliminated; it carried on underground. Matrona Nikonova, a simple, blind woman who lived in Moscow during the Soviet period until her death in the Stalin era in 1952, was one of these holy fools. She was marginalized from society but always prayed—especially during war—for the salvation of Russia. She exercised a ministry of compassion and intercession for the sick and suffering. Such a figure, a poor woman who had the gift of clairvoyance and compassion, was completely out of tune with Soviet oppressive rationality. Nevertheless, among the Russian people, especially during the Second World War, it was said that Stalin himself secretly went to her to receive protection for Moscow from the German attacks by her prayers. (There are small popular icons in which the saint is represented beside Stalin.) Today her sanctuary in the Russian capital is a place of pilgrimage and the object of great devotion.

Men and women who become marginalized to the point of seeming mad embody the wisdom of the cross in a Christian society. This is how the Archimandrite Spiridon describes a meeting with a fool for Christ in his native village at the end of the nineteenth century; wisdom and strangeness were mixed in the words of this man, who was regarded by many as a saint. The man told him: "They say I am mad, but my dear, without madness you cannot enter the kingdom of God. . . . As long as people are reasonable and sensible, the kingdom of God will not come upon earth."[3]

Becoming a Foreigner in Your Own Country

Some aspects of this foolishness for Christ are found in the peculiar case of Archimandrite Feodor Bucharev, who was born in Russia in 1824 and died in 1871. Bucharev was a learned monk. He belonged to the class of well-educated, intellectual clergy and was the author of theological works that had aroused interest and discussion. Young and widely known in church circles, he had good prospects of a promising career. After fifteen years of monastic life and theological study, he asked to be restored to lay status. This decision caused sharp controversy, but despite much pressure the ecclesiastical authorities were unable to change his mind. Such a step was by no means easy in tsarist Russia, because it condemned him to becoming a pariah in that society with its strong links between church and State. From the legal viewpoint his restoration to lay status was a "punishment," which branded him in such a way that it became difficult for him to find publishers for his works and a means of support. By his choice Bucharev marginalized himself. He did not consider that becoming a layman was a reduction to something less honorable than a monk. It was a choice that had its own theological logic. After giving up his monastic vows and his clerical status, he married in church. He declared that marriage was a choice of equal dignity with monastic celibacy.

Bucharev had led a respected life as an intellectual and a monk. Now he began to live a lay life among common people, while still keeping the monastic spirit. He regarded this choice as right for him: "In the witness to 'life in Christ' borne by Christians in difficult earthly conditions lies the royal priesthood of all the baptized, glorious and painful at the same time," writes Elisabeth

Behr-Sigel, who was among the first in the West to reflect on the significance of Bucharev's choice.[4]

Bucharev's life was not without grave difficulties in addition to his humiliation by the ecclesiastical authorities who had opposed his choice. Together with his wife he endured extreme poverty, loneliness, and the painful experience of the death of their only child. He had few friends who stood by him to the end. These witnessed to his serene simplicity and humility in a lay life that was anything but easy. His choice was to be among the marginalized, common people, kenotically living the mystery of the presence of Christ:

> Joining with Christ today means following him by descending into this hell with only the weapons of faith, hope and compassionate love. Neither crusade against the modern world, nor flee from it, nor kneel down before it. But inner light. . . . That could be the task for men of action and thought, who would at the same time be men of contemplation.[5]

For many of his contemporaries Bucharev had committed spiritual suicide by his restoration to lay status and condemning himself to a hard, marginalized life, renouncing the opportunities offered him by his ecclesiastical position. However, according to others, he was living in the spirit of the fools for Christ, marginalized in the church and society, whose existence had a prophetic value. Suicide or prophecy? That always remains the question about the lives of the fools for Christ at any period. According to Paul Evdokimov, Bucharev, by his paradoxical choice, became the initiator of "lay monasticism" in the modern world, among the common people, without being afraid of becoming marginalized from the church's circles and institutions.[6] Bucharev was a Christian who immersed himself in his time, trying to understand its signs and directions from the standpoint of a marginalized life. His life was a foolishness that became a prophecy for Christians in the contemporary world, showing that even there a life of deep faith can be lived, a true monasticism.

The Russian Church Seen from Siberia

The story of Archimandrite Spiridon is also significant. He was a Russian, born in 1875, who lived through the painful experience of the First World War and the Bolshevik Revolution. From his youth he had searched for God in a deep and intense way that was not without its moments of crisis and falling short. He became a monk and a priest, developing a strong critical awareness of the Russian church and hierarchy because of their links with power and money and also their sanctification of war.

That awareness grew in Spiridon during a life lived on the margins of the Russian Empire, in Siberia, in contact with the most marginalized people.

In the last decade of the nineteenth century quite a few Russians were impelled to leave their own homes to engage in the search for God in the monastic world or in pilgrimage, between the Holy Land and Mount Athos, but also on a mission to Siberia, which the Russian Empire was then colonizing. This spiritual movement also involved Spiridon. While has was still a layman he devoted himself to preaching to the Siberian population, knowing the very difficult situation of the local people from the spiritual and human point of view, but also the impossible conditions of life for prisoners and the deported. He met and listened to these marginalized people and became convinced that the life of Russian Christians who came to Siberia was often a scandal for the local people, who saw it as contradictory to the Christian message.

In Siberia, Spiridon realized the force of the gospel message he preached, but he also felt compassion for those living in this lonely, forsaken land. Life on this vast Russian margin, with the ambiguities of colonization and great poverty, radically changed him. He was particularly affected by the state of the prisoners and deportees, for example, by one of the Old Believers who initially mocked him and his preaching. But up to a point this man was deeply moved by Spiridon's tenderness:

You have struck me deeply—he told him—because in such a great sinner, the lowest of those sentenced to hard labor, you have discovered a man and what a man! A child of God! Everyone despises us, everyone regards us as abominable creatures and we even hate ourselves. . . . But you, you regard us quite differently. Know, Father, how sweet it is for us to be regarded as human beings! In fact, perhaps we are animals, but nevertheless we are human! Why do they despise us? Oh, Father, if everyone treated us like you, believe me, there would no longer be criminals on earth. Evil is only overcome by good. . . . From childhood I have never heard a good word from anyone.[7]

There are many stories of suffering and marginalized people that Spiridon tells in his memoirs of the Siberian mission. In this forsaken world he experienced the force of the word of the gospel, of forgiveness and mercy. To one prisoner who had rejected the church and who felt betrayed by priests, who cursed and regarded himself as cursed, Spiridon said:

"Remember Christ: he did not curse the world that crucified him, but prayed for it. When we curse people, this is a sign of our impotence and the weakness of our powers."[8]

A heretic who had seen him preaching and was struck by his tenderness to all, independent of their condition and the choices they had made, asked him in tears:

> "Why don't the priests say all this? If they taught us to understand the gospel well, our life would be transformed. I have listened to you more than once and have seen more than once how you treat the prisoners. . . . For you they are all equal and you are a real brother, a brother to all."[9]

On the extreme human margin of life in Siberia for prisoners and the deported, but also in the difficult conditions for the local population, Spiridon felt bitterly the deep contradictions of Russian Christianity, which, even in these lands, advanced with imperial power and the force of a state church, rather than with humanity and kindness. From this margin, even though it was his own peculiar viewpoint, he came to a better and painful understanding of the limits of the Russian church. A Buddhist lama who heard him preach said to him:

> "That is what Christ taught, but you Christians are not like that. You behave like wild beasts. You should be ashamed of talking about Christ, your mouth is all smeared with blood. Among us there

is nobody who lives worse than the Christians. For who commits fraud, lives a dissolute life, robs, lies and kills the most? The Christians."[10]

The lama recalls that with the building of the Trans-Siberian Railway, the Russian navvies came. They were drunk and violent with the local women; they stole and abuses became more widespread than ever before. In the light of this contradictory situation Spiridon asked himself: "Are we Christians ourselves really the true enemies of Christian preaching?"[11] Looked at from these margins, Christianity can be seen expanding and grasping from the center with pride and aggression, but without any real capacity for merciful attraction. From the Siberian margin, this upside-down world inhabited by the unfortunate, Spiridon realized the drama of the church and the country on the eve of the revolution:

Our whole land of Russia—he writes—is thick with churches, monasteries, chapels of all sorts, but when we look at our lives, then we look in vain for excuses, we have to admit that not only are we not Christians, but we never have been and we do not even know what Christianity is! Still we must not despair. . . . I am convinced that God loves Russia and will never let her die.[12]

Archimandrite Spiridon's trust in God's love for his country was not a form of nationalism. He had become aware of the weakness of Russian Christianity and dreamed of a profound renewal. Spiridon was changed by contact with this poor, marginal world. He became a conscientious priest, true to the gospel. In the years that followed his special character emerged strongly. Spiridon did not accept the sacralization of war in the First World War, which was proclaimed by the Orthodox religious authorities in the name of Holy Russia. Later, he did not even bend to Soviet power, despite its violence and harsh antireligious persecution.

In Kiev he led an important Orthodox brotherhood composed of intellectuals, students, and also poor people who assembled around his special liturgical ceremonies (in which he introduced some innovations, frowned upon by the hierarchy, like celebration with the doors of the iconostasis open). This was the Fraternity of Most Sweet Jesus. During the time he spent in Kiev, Spiridon was also very close to the poor. "It was not possible—he writes—not to have an attitude of compassion for those unfortunate workers, who after a hard day's work came to spend the night on a bunk in the dormitory."[13] During the First World War, when contact with the wounded and dead on the front overwhelmed him, he always sought out the marginalized to be with and to see life from the viewpoint of their sufferings.

Spiridon died in 1930, with the Soviet period in full swing, when many churches were closed, many priests arrested, religious life harshly repressed, and there were a growing number of martyrs for the faith. At his death hundreds of poor people accompanied his coffin in a very well-attended funeral. During the celebration a disciple of his remembered him as a priest of the marginalized and the poor.

> More than anything else your heart was attracted to the unfortunate, the humiliated and suffering people. More than anything else you loved to preach in attics and cellars in the midst of people worn out with heavy woes, where altar servers avoided going and where they met you at first with diffidence, then with amazement and finally with love.[14]

A Nun in the Camp

A better-known story is that of Elisabetta Skobtsova, a nun with the name Mother Maria. She also chose to be one of these fools for the world of the marginalized. This was the adventure of a woman who came from nineteenth-century Russia, from an aristocratic background, and with an artistic sensibility. She went through the years of the Bolshevik Revolution and ended up exiled in France, where she underwent a deep conversion to the faith of the Orthodox Church. In the 1920s she reached Paris, where there were many Russian exiles. These geographical facts do not explain the life story of this passionate, genuine, complex personality who ended up in monastic life after many intellectual and emotional vicissitudes.

Her life has many different chapters. It was a life in which people from the Russia of Nicholas II crossed with people from the world of the Bolshevik and revolutionary struggles. In 1920 the future Mother Maria went into exile from Russia, which nevertheless remained her spiritual home. Her pilgrimage continued until 1923, when she arrived in France with her second husband. Here, amid the Christian activity of Russian students, the Saint-Serge Institute of Orthodox Theology (founded in 1924), and personalities such as Bulgakov, Berdyaev, and Lev Gilet, she matured in her Christian identity. This was characterized by a deep thirst for genuineness, which she expressed in an original and paradoxical way by her decision to become a nun.

Mother Maria's particular kind of monasticism had blossomed with her pain at the death of her daughter: "I feel that my daughter's death forces me to become a mother of all," she declared. Metropolitan Eulogio, a great figure in emigrant Russian Christianity, told her at the time of her consecration as a nun: "There is more love, more humility and more need for you to remain in the backwaters of the world breathing that foul air." Mother Maria, a nun on the margins of the world, was a true nun. She dressed in a Russian black nun's habit (often stained by domestic work), and with the typical nun's headdress, but she did not withdraw from difficult situations or the poor.

In the West, Mother Maria radically rediscovered Orthodox Christianity and became a nun, living in the world and among the poor, both Russian immigrants and poor Parisians. That was unusual in the Russian monastic tradition. This special nun was deeply moved by the wretched poverty of so many people, which seemed to her to be a call to lead a different life. Her house-convent became a place of hospitality for many people wounded by life. There was no lack of liturgy in it, but life in her house was not at all regular according to the classical monastic canons. Mother Maria was imbued with spiritual freedom in her search for God and her love for men and women.

In 1935, Father Lev Gillet, an Orthodox priest (converted from Catholicism), went to live in Mother Maria's house-convent, where monastic life was combined with her family life and the fortunes of the poor. This is how he describes that environment: "It was a strange pandemonium, we had girls, fools, the evicted, unemployed."[15] Mother Maria, though keen to help everyone, recalls that it is not enough to develop all those social activities:

> An authentic social Christianity should not only have a Christian form. It must also be effectively Christian. For this it needs another dimension, a mystical foundation capable of pulling it out of a two-dimensional, flat spirituality and moralism and taking it to the depths of a multi-dimensional spirituality.[16]

Mother Maria believed that social action, or rather love for the marginalized, had to be based upon mysticism. Otherwise, it degenerates into voluntarism and easily burns itself out: "The great, the single initiator of action in the world—which is a real ascesis—is Christ, the Son of God who became incarnate in the world, wholly, without any holding back of his divinity."[17] For her, mysticism was the key to love for the poor:

> Social work, any dialogue with someone in the name of Christ, must be this liturgy outside the church. . . . Otherwise, even if we refer to Christian morality, our action will only be apparently Christian.[18]

The poor, the marginalized of Paris, the Russian immigrants, the persecuted Jews—all were this nun's friends.

Mother Maria looked at the Russian Orthodox Church of her Paris exile and dreamed that from this poverty and freedom a profound renewal might occur in it: "Our mission is to show that a free church can work miracles. And if we took our new, free, creative, bold spirit, back to Russia, our aim would be reached."[19] From the margin of the exiles, from the experience of diaspora, a renewal could come for the Mother Country.

The passionate and dramatic story of Mother Maria is emblematic of a reestablished communion between Christians (think of her openness to other denominations) in life and love for the poor and persecuted. Maria felt the drama of the divisions between Christians in relation to the Second World War and the evil project embedded in the conflict. Division among Christians weakened their voice in the face of evil. Maria, who was horrified by war, was certain that the conflict was preparing "the way for the next war, inexorably." Through her contact with the marginalized world she developed an original reading of the catastrophe striking Europe.

However, she realized that it was in time of war that there is "a unique chance for humanity today." She realized that "the war is an appeal; the war is what opens our eyes." Indeed, according to Mother Maria, the war, which dramatically concentrates all evils and is the mother of all poverties, demands a single, decisive, mobilization of all spiritual energies together with a simple and radical realization of the goal of unity for all Christians in the world.

In 1943, in Paris occupied by the Nazis, her son Yuri and Father Dimitri, a Russian priest who worked with her, ended up in the hands of the Gestapo. Mother Maria looked for them and tried to get them freed. She was arrested herself and deported to Ravensbrück. Her crime was solidarity with the Jews. Her old mother told the Gestapo officer who searched the house-convent where the persecuted were hidden: "My daughter is a Christian. For her there is neither Jew nor Greek, but only people in danger. If you were in trouble she would also help you." The Germans sought to smash the activity of this woman, who had also helped a group of Jewish children flee from the Velodrome, where those to be deported were gathered before being interned. She was accused of helping Jews to hide.

In the Nazi camp at Ravensbrück, Maria behaved with dignity and serenity in the face of the inhuman treatment meted out to the deported. On Good Friday, March 31, 1945, she was selected for the gas chamber. This friend of the marginalized and persecuted in Paris died in the concentration camp, which in those years represented Europe's extreme margin.

Mother Maria's life was frequently marked by war (the First and Second World Wars and also the Russian civil war), and it ended at the heart of the twentieth century in the concentration camp. Her final messages from the camp were an embroidered veil representing victory over evil and an icon, also embroidered, with the crucified Christ in his mother's arms. They witness to a life that in the great suffering and forsakenness of the camp believed in the resurrection of Jesus and celebrated it.

A Twentieth-Century Roman Fool for Christ

Western Christianity has had far fewer fools for Christ, people who remove themselves to the margins of church and social life. Perhaps we should look more deeply into the centuries-old tradition of hermits, some expressions of Franciscanism, and other initiatives. But we would always end up finding that the church of Rome tends progressively to regulate the lifestyles that develop on its margins.

However, there is one story, largely unknown but still striking, precisely because it started in Rome during the 1940s. That was when the church of Pius XII was involved in the clash with communism in Italy, while Eastern Europe was unleashing a persecution of Christians under its Marxist regimes. This is the story of Giuseppe Sandri, who was ordained a priest in 1928. He was learned and sophisticated, a handsome man, destined for a brilliant career in the church. His deep culture was shown in various studies and in translations of the scriptures. In 1949 Sandri requested and obtained permission to return to lay status from the ecclesiastical authorities. In some ways his story recalls that of Bucharev in the nineteenth century and other fools for God.

The reasons for his laicization are unusual for a Catholic priest. It was not a punishment imposed by the authorities, nor was it a matter of his desire to marry. He was restored to lay status "in order to be able to live the gospel better" and "to preach the gospel of Jesus Christ better." These motives were incongruous and incomprehensible for the Catholic Church mentality of the time. Don Giuseppe De Luca, a Roman priest and learned scholar, was a great friend of Sandri's. He did not fully understand Sandri's decision and initially opposed his abandonment of the priesthood. He felt it was a betrayal. But after a time Don De Luca had to admit that his friend's life was a mystery that could not be judged simply. He wrote: "Close to him a new feeling for the Christian life arises in your heart, and makes you yourself seem like a pure formality, not just the things you do, including the Mass, but the spirit in which you do them."[20]

By his option for a life on the margins of the church and its institutions, Sandri wanted to show how an overvaluation of the institutional church had developed within Catholicism. He lived the life of the poor, like a pilgrim, and devoted himself in a quiet way to translating the scriptures into a language accessible to the people. This is what he said in a conversation in 1976 that was recorded without his knowledge:

> I became a Christian four years after I had become a priest: I did not leave the church, because I feel Christian, through and through. . . . I had this feeling I should return to base and speak about my faith, one to one with my fellow Christians and others independently of rank, which at that period had a certain halo of authority.[21]

According to Romana Guarnieri, who was his friend, like Don De Luca, Sandri often discussed with De Luca the value of priesthood, and how by their lives priests had become distanced from the gospel model. To Sandri, ecclesiastical Rome looked like a contradiction. Guarnieri recalls a time during the 1940s when they were talking about Cardinal Suhard of Paris and the worker priests. Sandri showed great interest and was well informed about them, even attracted by this new way of living as a priest, whereas De Luca considered it to be a novelty without any future.[22] Sandri's decision created a sensation in the ecclesiastical environment of Pius XII's Rome: "It seems he goes about saying strange things: that now it is time to begin living with the freedom of the children of God," says a note sent to the Vicariate in 1949.[23]

So Giuseppe Sandri became a vagabond apostle, tramping through the mountains or the countryside or the city margins, always without a settled home. He did not have an official residence. He rarely revisited Rome, where those who welcomed him noted that his life was one of great austerity and penance. De Luca wrote about Sandri:

> Where he went there was no electric light and that evening there was not even the usual candle stub; so he ate at the door under starlight. Then he lay down and I sensed that he was feverish. Certainly he was lying on the ground. That was our dear and tremendous Sandri.[24]

On the other hand, Guarnieri relates:

> Someone had given him some clothes, worker's clothes with a pair of wooden clogs for his feet. It was rumored that he worked as a quarryman in a quarry on the outskirts of Rome and slept in an abandoned barn.[25]

Ennio Francia describes him thus:

> It was not known where he lived, what and how he ate, how he managed to drag through a life that,

however wretched, had to be got through. . . . He had become so out of touch that, when he asked for a card to vote against abortion and divorce, he had laboriously to reconstruct his family status and demonstrate that he was still alive. He did not live anywhere but turned up everywhere, in big cities and in remote country. On Sundays he went into a village, heard Mass, made up a bundle of supplies and returned to the hills. And he sang the praises of the Lord at the top of his voice, because he knew that only "the Father" heard him. And what did he do? He taught the catechism to children and builders: and he talked with the dockers. He had friends everywhere, and in order to speak better about the "Father" to them he studied Greek deeply.[26]

Small groups of lay people gathered round him, ordinary people, married (among other things Sandri strongly stressed the value of marriage, which, in his opinion, was belittled by the ecclesiastical mentality). In a letter to a woman friend he stressed how, through its integration with the empire, the church had opted for a logic of power and had introduced "natural religiosity" to make the ecclesiastical community accessible to the masses: "The church becomes powerful and rich, bishops are raised to functions that include very important civil and administrative functions, everything changes color and tone."[27] In his opinion the parish was a form of church life that was now in crisis:

> Your drama about the parish was what in the early centuries gave rise to the religious orders. It is a drama of the whole church then and always. And it is basically the same drama which in some cases gave rise to schisms and heresies. The structure becomes flabby; it gives way and becomes worldly. Then some people withdraw, some people reject it; others do not reject the unity and the structure but still withdraw. The parish is the last outpost of unity and structure, however crushed and debased it may be.[28]

Nevertheless, Sandri did not want to leave the church or its unity; he accepted obedience to it, even when he found it incomprehensible. Neither did he reject the parish; he did not plan to reform it or preach reform. But he was a man who lived a life of poverty as a vagabond:

> Christians may well see where the hierarchy has gone wrong, and how the essential faith of the early Christians has become mixed up with the promotion of values and meanings that are also legitimate but always secondary. They may well understand the need for church renewal. However, they still

love the church assembly and want to be members
of it, and if possible not unworthy ones.[29]

Sandri charged the church with a degeneration into
clericalism, which had happened over the centuries, indeed, with the formation of a real "clerical caste," which
no longer had any living relationship with what was for
him the Christian community modeled on the Acts of
the Apostles and Paul's letters. (His translation of these
was read by his friends and disciples.) For him, the real
Christian community was the "assembly" of Jesus's disciples, as he called it.

From his marginal position Sandri also followed Vatican II: "The council must renew deeply," he observed.
But he was critical of the council renewal of the 1960s-
1970s, the bureaucratization of the church, and also
its progressive Catholic theology and pastoralism—he
who had quit the hierarchical church of Pius XII. He
declared that the Italian Bishops Conference—we are
in the post-conciliar years—had become a bureaucracy
and the living sense of the bishop's relationship with
the "assembly" had been lost.[30] After the council the
most worrying aspect in the church for him was not the
Vatican old men—as he called the cardinals and Curia
officials—during the years of Paul VI. In 1974, at the
time of the referendum on the law that had introduced
divorce, Sandri took a firm position, among his friends,

voting yes for the repeal of the law.[31] The crisis in religious practice after the council seemed to him like the decadence of natural religion, which is different from Christianity.

> I am not talking about the usual lot . . . chronic and almost stylized figures of most noble agnostics who weave panegyrics and break bread in which they don't believe. . . . I am speaking about the dozens of priests aged between thirty and forty, who don't know who Jesus Christ is and explain the gospel with the hand-outs of Bultmann and Jeremias.[32]

It is difficult to trace a profile of Sandri because—despite some writings with limited circulation and some almost furtively collected conversations—he did not like talking about himself. He was very shy, almost clandestine in society. Commenting on the parable of the treasure in the field, Sandri in some way illustrated the life he had chosen:

> With this discovery he is happy, so happy . . . and he goes and sells everything he has. Also the "madness" . . . (it is impossible that someone invented the parable, it belongs to the one speaking). The madness of the person who discovers the treasure, hides it and goes to sell everything, sells everything,

house, shirt, everything, why? Because this treasure is worth more than anything.[33]

His choice, which he also proposed to his friends, was to read the Gospels, changing his own life and exhorting others to read the Gospels and practice the gospel message. That is how Giuseppe Sandri's life developed, a life on the margins of poverty and renunciation, until his death in 1985. A seminary companion wrote about his end:

They say that Giuseppe Sandri went off in his own way, a solitary way, in a hut in the Salerno district that a pious fellow seminarian had offered him for his use. As they did not see him come out for several days the peasants went to look for him and found him burning with fever.[34]

What is most people's judgment of Sandri? The documentation gathered by the Rome Vicariate at the time he left the priesthood says: "Some thought he was mad; most people said he was a saint." The Cardinal Vicar of Rome, Francesco Marchetti Selvaggiani, observed: "I incline to hold that Sandri was affected by mental unbalance, caused by his vagabond life, and the exaggerated and strange privations to which he voluntarily subjected himself."[35] Sandri left a legacy of silence about his life: "If anyone asks you who was Sandri, answer: Who? Sandri? He was someone who loved Jesus. That's all."[36] This is often the choice of those who opt for the margins and a hidden life. Their motive is a sense of fruitfulness that they believe goes far beyond their personal fame or the memory of their story.

4

Mission on the Margins

The Growth of Contemporary Margins

In the twentieth century Christianity was confronted
forcefully with new margins, not places that afforded
an opportunity for seeking God in a life of faithfulness,
but rather spaces where the survival of Christianity was
actually under threat. These margins represented a "new
land" even in societies with a long continuous history of
Christianity. From the nineteenth century on the industrial revolution concentrated a mass proletariat of workers in the cities where they were engaged in industry.
This led to the building of new housing on the margins
of the city, often marked by dire living conditions and
sparse services. The new margins or poor suburbs often
seemed like the cities of the poor, about which John
Chrysostom preached in his homilies on Antioch.

The urbanization of the masses and hence the growth
of city margins or suburbs, along with the progressive

depopulation of the rural areas or their conversion into new sprawling suburbs, has been a constant characteristic of contemporary history. While the country districts lose inhabitants, the modern city "gobbles up" the margins and outlying districts. Thus the city margins or suburbs are often inhabited by marginalized people who are excluded from the wealth of the city while they serve its needs and labor requirements.

Over the centuries the Catholic Church has developed a juridical-pastoral relationship with these territories. During the twentieth century the whole globe was mapped out in ecclesiastical districts to provide the faithful with pastoral care wherever they lived, whether in greater or lesser density. This is shown in the *Atlas hierarchicus.* There is no corner (figuratively speaking) of the earth that does not belong to a diocese and an ecclesiastical area with an official pastor. The diocese is then broken down into small ecclesiastical units, the parishes. These care for the faithful in a particular area and are organized around one or more churches. In mission areas (those controlled by the Roman Congregation for the Evangelization of Peoples), where the church has been set up more recently, the diocesan/parish structure is rather fuzzier, although the model is the same. But in the areas of ancient Christendom, the church's organizational outreach covers the whole territory, like the administration of a State. This parish-based situation is weakened and up for discussion today because of the lack of priests. Such a structural organization expresses a statist and, I would say, imperial vision. Its main relationship is with the territory. The term *diocese* (administration) was developed from the administrative areas of the Roman Empire.

We could say that there is no place excluded from the geography of the church, which embraces the whole globe. It is a Roman idea of geographical control, with named responsible officials—bishops, priests, and so on—through whom the church covers each part of its ecclesiastical area.

Nevertheless, the tumultuous population growth at the margins has caused a crisis for this Roman vision of the church. Often in a marginal area the parish is a "citadel" for the church, standing within an environment beset by secularization, distant from the ancient rural religious connections, or with many immigrants who are not Catholics. The parish is no longer the heart of the village. In the past the church was the center of village social life. It was surrounded by a graveyard and stood for an ordered Christian universe. The parish on the margins, sometimes set in a corner of the area, no longer has its traditional central position in the square where social and public life takes place. Indeed, the central position of the church in the village and the cathedral in the city center is a manifestation of a Christendom that is now over, even in countries with an ancient Christian tradition.

The religious fabric in the historic cities was characterized not only by parishes but by a complex interweaving of Christian life, from the confraternities with their churches, oratories, and religious houses for both men and women, and various works. The church, at the center of the city or the village, was accompanied by the host of religious and pastoral institutions that permeated Christian society. Sometimes the ancient churches remain, but the society has changed and is no longer only Christian but religiously pluralistic, and the socio-religious references of the past have been lost. Today's Christian institutions are an isolated reality in the social context. The world of the Catholic faithful, reduced in number and socially distinct, is restricted to the parish environment, just one component of a pluralistic society.

Under these circumstances most of the faithful become unfaithful, as Cardinal Montini, archbishop of Milan, observed. He was thinking of Italy in the 1950s.[1] The church remains the world of the devout, often a different world from that of the masses on the margins, who are the majority. New and difficult working conditions have caused profound changes in the mentality of what used to be called the working class. We have already mentioned the effect of the socialist movement in this environment. Of course, not all the men and women living on the margins are working class, but these marginal areas are strongly marked by a working-class mentality, which causes a growing alienation from the world and ceremonies of the church. As has already been said, the great problem for the church in the twentieth and twenty-first centuries has been its relationship with the margins. It is finding them increasingly impenetrable, especially those urban and working-class areas that the church feels are hostile and alien to it.

Estrangement from Christianity

This brings us back to the question raised in a significant way in Corbon's reply to Bishop Dupanloup, who asked, "Who will tell me why these people abandon us?" At the end of the nineteenth century the church realized that the people, or many of them, were abandoning Catholic institutions and the Christian faith. This was especially the case with the proletarian world, which was undergoing a profound transition on the margins of cities and in industrial labor. It was not just a matter of alienation from ecclesiastical institutions; new expectations also were turning the proletarian world toward movements other than the church.

The liberation of the marginalized working-class masses no longer came from hopes and consolations offered by the church, which was often considered an ally of the rich and powerful. Liberation was sought in self-organization by the working class and its own capacity to struggle and better itself, that is, in the socialist and communist movement. The liberation struggle of the working class through political parties, trade unions—movements that often looked to socialist or Marxist ideology—is a long story that cannot be summed up in a few lines. It is another universe of ideas and values, in which religious faith and the church have no place or are considered in a negative light. And it is a universe that is often in conflict with the church and the movements linked to it. That was the church's great problem in Europe throughout the twentieth century.

The story of the margins intersects with the story of socialism and "new" politics that have at times assumed the character of a messianic salvation of the proletarian masses. During this process, which lasted more than a century, we do not need to think that the church was static or shut away in its parish citadel or institutions, rigidly blocked off. An important Catholic social and working-class movement arose at the end of the nineteenth century in the wake of Leo XIII's *Rerum novarum*. In fact, there was a vast and varied social Catholicism in the nineteenth and twentieth centuries, sometimes in competition with the working-class movement. But the spirit of liberation—especially on the margins—tended to breathe strongest in the socialist movement.

In marginal areas workers and their families were often abandoned. Nineteenth-century novels often depict the privations of the proletariat, family dramas, hard working conditions, and exploitation of children as workers. The first sociological inquiries into work and the workers' environment show the dire conditions of life on the margins and in industrial jobs. In this new and difficult situation there was a progressive detachment of the masses from religious life—the secularization of the marginalized (who also sometimes lived in slum areas in city centers). *Secularization* was a fashionable expression in sociology and in pastoral studies in the twentieth century. The term describes the phenomenon of de-Christianization and autonomy from church regulation. It was a complex movement that questioned certain beliefs and traditional loyalties, and it especially meant detachment from a social life regulated by religion.

At any rate, the world of Christendom, whether urban or rural, was now over. During the nineteenth and twentieth centuries the bourgeoisie also became secularized, imbued with positivist, scientific, or liberal culture. At the same time—following a different route—there was the secularization of the lower classes.[2] It involved the whole city, which now became a secular reality.[3] Progressively, urban culture molded the whole of society; in more recent times this has been accelerated with the development of the mass media.

As we have already said, the marginalized, especially the proletariat, organize themselves in a struggle for their own liberation. At the heart of the nineteenth century Pierre Proudhon forcefully proclaimed the ir-religion of a working class liberating itself with its own hands:

> The people no longer bow to us, and although it is impossible for them to follow the chain of ideas and facts by reason. . . . Their instincts tell them that the only thing preventing them being happy and rich through their labor is theology. At heart they are no longer Christian.[4]

We have already spoken about what Olivier Clément aptly describes as the divorce between the sacrament of the altar (religious life) and the sacrament of the poor; that is, the separation between the church and the world of the poor and marginalized, between the faith and their struggles.

Naturally, this process of secularization of the expectations and hopes of the marginalized is complex and varied. It depends on the circumstances in various countries and differs in accordance with different economies and histories, and it has various cycles and movements. However, one of the great dramas of twentieth-century Christianity was the alienation of large groups of the population from the practice of Christian communities and religion.

However, the margins become important in the social and political life of the new political parties, especially with the increase in the number of voters with the advent of universal suffrage. The church struggles to follow this model, with many of its initiatives linked to a campaign culture but within a perspective of Christendom. They are developed on a territorial and parochial basis, even though they also involve associations and specialized movements. Often there is a tendency to reconstruct a "little Christendom" around Christian institutions or in the parish. The outlook of the city is largely and increasingly secular, both among the marginalized and the wealthy, in contact with new lifestyles and a nonreligious culture.

Sociological studies register a profound change that has now come about: a great crisis of contemporary religiosity. Secularization has become the everyday outlook on life, while faith and religious practice seem to have been brushed into a corner or become just a small part of social life. This is a great change in the religious history of Europe. Within the working class the change often means not only secularization, but a loss of the symbols and rites of Christendom. The new myths and rites are those of political struggle and liberation from being marginalized. René Rémond, a great French historian, among the finest investigators of contemporary Christianity, very acutely writes about the relationship between the church and the working-class world:

> The root cause of the divorce between the working-class world and the church lies in a difference of mentality. Two cultures have grown up side by side but alien to one another. Whether this happened by chance or was predestined, the irreversible fact is that the working class has become aware of itself in an intellectual world that excludes the religious dimension, at least the one that Christianity represented.[5]

Paris and a Concerned Cardinal

Reflection on the "new lands" of the margins, especially in the twentieth century, may appear too generalized if it is not focused at least on the history of a particular urban environment. Paris suggests itself because it is a great European metropolis, one that has undergone an intense process of industrialization and urbanization since the eighteenth century. The Catholic Church has a strong presence there, unlike other great European cities, such as London, which also saw the growth of an urban proletariat but where Catholics are a minority of the population. For the French capital, secularization has obvious roots in the French Revolution. Despite the political and religious restoration, the regime of Christendom was never restored.

Moreover, its history between the nineteenth and twentieth centuries was turbulent, one reason being that the working class became protagonists. During the 1848 revolution, in the clash between the government and working-class forces, the archbishop of Paris, Monseigneur Afre, was killed when he came to try to mediate. Two decades later, in 1871, the city was the theater for the Paris Commune uprising, drenched in blood. During these events the archbishop of Paris, Monseigneur Darboy, was shot by the communards.

Even in the twentieth century, in Paris as in other cities, the urban scenario was not yet fully realized by the church as a viewpoint from which to restructure itself in a new way. In many countries Catholicism survived without becoming aware of the changes, defending the tradition of Christendom, claiming to be the sole voice of religious life. In other countries it restricted its horizon to traditional ecclesiastical structures and institutions, making them small islands of Christendom in a plural and secularized society.

This process of transition from a "believing people" within a framework of Christendom (with all its varieties and differences in belonging and practice) to a restricted ecclesiastical community was accompanied by the loss of a global vision of Christianity and its horizon. The global vision is the city in all its components, including those that do not relate to the church but to which the church feels it should reach out. The church always considered itself to be the church of the city, but with a complex view and a sense of responsibility for the whole, even when the whole population was not Catholic. From the diocesan center emanated the pastoral and religious government of the city, which spread over the whole urban society and the surrounding country areas, which were part of the episcopal territory. But one of the effects of the process of secularization—though not everywhere—was a retreat of the church into its own institutions, as a minority whose outlook did not extend over the whole city.

The story of Catholicism in Paris is interesting and special. It could be said that the French capital is exemplary for the encounter, beset with conflicts, crises, and difficulties between Catholicism and modernity throughout the nineteenth and twentieth centuries. As a result, the Parisian church underwent a period of significant change.

Emmanuel Suhard was cardinal archbishop from 1940 to 1949. These were the difficult years of war and German occupation, followed by reconstruction and the Cold War. The cardinal was a crucial figure for understanding the reality of the urban world, in which the church had a new kind of mission.

In a 1947 pastoral letter, *Essor ou déclin de l'Eglise,* Suhard inquired into the church's future in the modern city. "Today," he said of the church, "the apostasy of the masses points to its failure." The cardinal was strongly aware of the church's failure to deal with the falling away of the marginalized masses—a real apostasy. In 1943 Suhard wrote in his diary: "Our whole population no longer thinks in a Christian way. There is an abyss between it and the Christian communities. We need to get out of our house and walk among them."[6] These words are a note to himself, not written for a public speech. They show the sensitive awareness of one who has taken a complex situation to heart. The church must go out from its own environment and institutions and overcome the distance in order "to walk among them."

In some ways these words prefigure those of Pope Francis seventy years later. *Evangelii gaudium* stresses the point: we must go out and meet a world that no longer belongs to the faithful. The difference in time between the cardinal of Paris and the pope and the different situations to which they are referring show that it is a long-term problem. The church is not a minority that must take care of its doctrinal purity and defend itself in some way in a pluralist and relativist society. In its deepest vocation it is called to take on the whole city and act in it, well beyond the limits of its own environment. Neither is the church a minority that should wage cultural battles for unforsakable values in the media and public opinion, as minorities do today in the global society. The church's mission is to go out, far from its own home, and meet a world that has become distant. That, in short, is the pope's vision. In this sense he has reverted to a long-term question and placed it at the center of debate for the church.

The margins challenge the church. It is not enough to establish a presence with new parish buildings. The church needs to insert itself into the world of the marginalized, into their lives and culture. In order to enter these distant universes—humanly, rather than geographically distant—the church needs to go "out of its own home." That involves a change of mentality and style. The church must set off into a new way of living. Cardinal Suhard sadly confessed this conviction to a colleague:

> We are ten centuries behind, with a ten-century handicap. We have been surrounded with a whole lot of dross. We have become bourgeois. Ten centuries weighing on us. Some day or other, simply by evolution of the facts, we will be forced to return to gospel simplicity. We have adopted the faults of rulers. When I go into a working-class district I am ashamed.[7]

That feeling was also found among those close to the archbishop. We must break down the wall and fill up the abyss created by history. That was Archbishop Suhard's dream, especially when he became aware—with great distress—of the religious condition of the margins. During the years of his ministry he went about making his dream a reality through personal contacts and visits to marginal districts, the poor suburbs of Paris.

In *Les Saints vont en enfer,* a very successful novel based on the story of the worker-priests, Catholic writer Gilbert Cesbron recalls the end of the cardinal's life: "In his final weeks he left off his official audiences and daily duties performed over the past ten years, to have himself driven through the Paris suburbs in his shabby, old-fashioned small black car like a sexton." The cardinal looked at the faces of the people he met, "his pagan people," and said: "All God's children! And I am responsible for them all."[8] He had the feeling of a far-off, lost world, with which there was no contact. He also went to Sagny, a marginal working-class district. Dressed in black, he attended the mass of a worker-priest, held in the evening after work. But he left before the end so as not to create a disturbance. He was convinced it was necessary to enter the world on the margins, discreetly but decisively.

France, a Mission Country?

A study conducted by two priests, Henri Godin and Yves Daniel, had struck Cardinal Suhard forcefully. It was published in 1943 in a small book with the provocative title *La France, pays de mission?* [France, mission country?]. It was a question that contained a proposal: the church should become missionary in those worlds where it had now become irremediably marginal. It was driven by the realization that France—and Paris first and foremost—had become a mission country, like those countries which had only recently been evangelized. Using the term *mission country* for a country with an ancient Christian tradition was astonishing.

As the authors argued, the margins, where the proletariat live, was now a pagan world, while the ways of presenting the church were no longer suited to keeping people in live contact with it. Even if a parish was set in a marginal area and there were special associations for pastoral care of the working class, this created a "Catholic" environment around the institution. It barely communicated with the workers. They represented a different world. Together, parish and church were failing to be missionary on the margins.

That was the context for the creation of the Paris Mission and the France Mission, where priests were sent to live in a proletarian environment or were actually workers in factories, living like everybody else, in order to revitalize Christianity at the heart of this marginal world. These priests opted to live in a working-class environment; often they worked in factories or did simple manual work. Through their daily life and work they showed that it was possible to live as Christians in these areas where they tried to make the church accessible to all. As priests and workers they tried by their presence to show that it was possible to be Christians on the margins.

The Paris Mission, carried out mainly by worker-priests in the poor suburbs among the proletariat, was intimately linked with Cardinal Emmanuel Suhard, who wanted it and supported it until his death. Gilbert Cesbron related how Archbishop Suhard was not only the founder of the Paris Mission but a constant supporter of the worker-priests. This is attested by many sources; for example, Emile Poulat, a historian of these events and also a participant, relates that the worker-priests were welcomed to his house by the cardinal, without any appointment, at any time.[9] For Suhard, the worker-priests' mission was vital. What was at stake was the future presence of the church in the big city because—for him—the church had to start again from the margins.

It was not a question of extending the church's control or services more widely to new sectors of the margins. The challenge for the Paris Mission was to bring about the rebirth in these marginal areas of a church that felt distant, almost as if it belonged to other social classes and another world. In a beautiful way the cardinal expressed his idea of the church's mission in the big city in a homily in the Cathedral of Notre Dame, five months before his death. It is his vision of Paris, which he kept in its entirety, an expression of his sense of personal responsibility toward the whole city, without excluding any environment or area.

> I invite you to imagine yourselves standing with me before the Basilica of Montmartre and there, take a look! As far as your eyes can see there lies Paris, a city with grave disorders and a city of saints. Beneath those smoking roofs almost six million inhabitants live and move, love and quarrel, pray and despair. There lies the enormous city which God entrusted to me on loan. Why? To save it! Saving Paris means two things: saving souls and saving the city. . . . Woe is me if I do not preach the gospel, cries St Paul. Following Paul and standing here before you, I take up that terrible cry.[10]

A Brief Big Story

The worker-priest experience lasted a very short time. It ended in 1954 by order of Pius XII. Nevertheless, it was intense and significant. The lives of these priests in the poor suburbs and in factories seemed to be at odds with their priestly identity. Therefore, by order of the Holy See, these priests had to give up their jobs. This brought to an end an episode that had caused much discussion but was strongly supported by Cardinal Suhard and some of the French bishops. By the time it ended in 1954 Suhard was already dead. Rome knew that quite a few of the worker-priests had sided against the government and the bosses or had demonstrated with the vigorous left-wing peace movement. By so doing, weren't they collaborators with international communism, which the pope had condemned and which persecuted Christians in Eastern Europe? Weren't they betraying their Christian world by collaborating with the church's enemies?

According to Rome, the worker-priests were too adapted to the lifestyle of the workers and the factories. They were adopting the working-class way of thinking and behaving and that of its political movements and trade unions. They were more closely identified with the proletariat than with the church. That accusation was rejected by the majority of these worker-priests, but so it appeared to Rome and to various sectors of French Catholicism. Moreover, for the pope, being workers and living a worker's life was endangering their priesthood. Pius XII declared it was no longer possible to continue this bold initiative on the knife-edge of two worlds. They could not settle so firmly on the margins; there was the risk of becoming estranged from the church.

Priests who had become workers and missionaries among the proletariat risked becoming marginal in the church. Besides, by setting themselves between two sometimes conflicting worlds, they were subject to tensions and contradictions that at that time were irresolvable. They were torn between two loyalties, to the church of their priesthood and their vocation, and to the working class whom they had opted for and lived among.

The era of the worker-priests lasted about ten years. Not long. Nevertheless, it is a big story of an attempt to bridge an abyss. Poulat, who took part in the Paris Mission during those years, noted that it was an attempt to go out from the Catholic ecclesiastical world to enter the world of the proletariat. The priests were inculturated into the marginal world and into the values and battles of the working class. They shared their sufferings and hopes and made contact with the social and political organizations for their self-liberation. That involved such a great change in their lives that—for Pius XII—their new lifestyle became incompatible with their Catholic priesthood or put their fundamental identity at risk. However—Poulat observed—it also forced a reconsideration of Catholicism by those on the left. The impact of these priests upon the working-class world caused a change in French communist opinion of Catholicism, which was no longer considered to be part of the enemy front that exploited the working class.

Although the experiment lasted a very short time, it was truly emblematic and achieved widespread fame in public opinion, not only in France. For example, a young Polish priest, Karol Wojtyla, coming from a solidly traditional Catholic world and sent by his bishop to study in Rome before the Polish frontiers were closed by communism, arrived in Paris in 1947 especially to study these new pastoral experiments. He met Cardinal Suhard and took great interest in the worker-priests. He was struck by this "return to the simplicity of the gospel," as he wrote two years later in a Catholic journal in Cracow. And he added: "The bald, radical statement that France is a mission country, has been the fruit of long and deep reflections. . . . It is not that easy to take on the responsibility implied in such a statement."[11]

Many objected, wondering how it was possible to define countries like France with such an ancient Christian history as pagan. That criticism circulated among the Roman Curia. But the young Wojtyla had grasped that this pastoral experiment reflected a new understanding of the reality and courageously took responsibility for it. These remarks by the future John Paul II show the international interest aroused by the worker-priests beyond the borders of France.

Certainly, the experiment had not reached its full fruition when it was brought to an end. The worker-priests did not live in parishes or in ecclesiastical institutions geographically close to the working-class world but in that world itself. They established new relationships with the people on the margins. They lived as workers, and that is what they felt themselves to be. They were fully embedded in that lifestyle. However, there were two different tendencies. There were those who stressed the need for the priests' presence in the factory where they would establish new friendships with working-class people, showing that in such a difficult environment, where they were struggling and exploited, it was still possible to believe. The priests worked like other workers. This could establish a Christian community based on that witness but outside the parish and institutional framework. That was a church reborn from the working-class margins.

Emile Poulat explains that this was the prevalent line among the worker-priests. Perhaps rather lyrically, the protagonist of Cesbron's novel, a priest working in a factory, expresses his identification with the working-class world: "In fact, it's enough to be there, with Christ in our heart—they feel that perfectly well!—a presence on the shop-floor that leaves nobody untouched." In this way the priest became a worker with the workers and marginal with the marginalized. He suffered all the distance of this marginal world from the rest of the city and also from the church's own structures. In short, this was a church reborn from the margins, within the framework of working-class life, with a poor and simple Christian community made up of marginalized people who were a long way from the Christian faith, sometimes hostile but above all alien to it.

Cesbron was moved by his personal experience of that environment

> as a young bourgeois can be who has never been poor, and suddenly discovers the conditions of the working class, the strikes, the unsanitary lodgings, the misfortunes, dismay, loneliness and at the same time the solidarity, the gospel lived out by people who do not even know the word "gospel" exists.[12]

For Cesbron, it was the overwhelming discovery of a world that was not geographically distant but humanly very far indeed from middle-class Paris. And where, he wondered, was the church?

In the novel Father André Depierre was a priest who had been in the Resistance during the Second World War. At the age of twenty-four he went to live in Montreuil, a wretchedly poor suburb in Paris, where he worked as a rag-and-bone man (but did not work in a factory like other Paris Mission priests). Depierre's idea was that it was necessary to create a community in a working-class environment. A new Christian way of life could be developed there: "What the people unconsciously expect from the church is hope." The church with its parish and associated structures was distant from the proletarian world, because it represented a different environment, a Catholic way of life close to the ecclesiastical world. It was like the parish belfry: "it tolled six times with a lost, indifferent sound." The church's institutions were alien to the working-class world. It was also a question of mentality and lifestyle.

For Father Depierre, it was not just a question of going out to meet a people who were far from God—which was the true aim—but there were also human and spiritual riches to discover and value among those people, who were distant from the church but who held important values. It was necessary to bring them to a Christian and community life within that environment and within their own cultural and human parameters. So, according to this priest, it was not just a question of bringing the gospel but also of receiving human riches and positive values like solidarity from these marginalized people.

Among the seventy thousand inhabitants of Montreuil, Depierre believed there were many "unconscious members of the church": people capable "of solidarity and a revolutionary mysticism." Therefore, the mission priest was not projecting the Christian message upon a tabula rasa, but upon human beings who also held values that sometimes were not to be found in the "city of the rich." André Depierre and his friends (lay people who formed a community with him) wanted to introduce a new interest in the church among the masses in a de-Christianized world: an "infectious curiosity, a collective and conscious appeal." There was an unconscious thirst for God among these marginalized people, often hidden by years of wretched poverty, abandonment, and humiliation.

The missionaries were not there to convert some isolated individuals to Christianity, taking them out of their own environment (into the Catholic world of the parish or Catholic organizations), but rather to create the church among the proletariat and marginalized, at the same time learning from the poorest. Thus a community arose in Montreuil, which was a reference point for a people's liturgy (celebrated in courtyards rather than in the parish church), for practical solidarity, education, and struggle for a home. This local people's Christian community was focused around the weekly Mass.

The local option taken by Depierre was not shared by all the worker-priests. Did the mission have its focal point in the city suburbs or in the factory? Didn't the factory represent the heart of this marginal world and the emblematic setting for its exploitation? How was one to enter the world of the proletariat? Depierre's position and that of the other priests represented two different options, but both were ways of being personally present on the margins. There was also a priest nicknamed Father Pigalle (called after the name of the famous Parisian entertainment place), who engaged in work with prostitutes.

Despite the difference, the action of the worker-priests and that of their lay collaborators was driven by a fundamental passion for the margins and the marginalized—a passion that led them outside the normal ecclesiastical framework. That is found only at particular moments in church history, like after Vatican II. It happened, for example, in Rome, where so many Catholics, especially young people, went into the poor suburbs and marginal areas in a burst of solidarity to share, help, and teach in schools. Even when things were most difficult, the worker-priests were driven by that passion for the margins and the will to make positive contact with the reality of the working-class world.

Marta Margotti, a scholar who has traced the history of the worker-priests from 1943 to 1954, observes that after a few years the "missionaries" dropped some of the strong convictions they had set out with—convictions of outsiders who regarded themselves as bringing in higher values:

The working-class world turned out to hold unsuspected positive values that were much richer from the spiritual point of view than what the missionaries had learnt during their seminary training or in Catholic associations. Hence, from their different approaches and experiences in the local areas and factories, the members of the Paris Mission gained the conviction that it was necessary to come to terms with this universe in ferment, to go with this now adult proletariat, and that the Christian community should deepen its roots into the "proletarian country, a single beloved country."[13]

We can imagine the stark clash between the proletarian world and the ecclesiastical culture of the worker-priests, trained in seminaries and coming from ecclesiastical institutions. The battles for peace, strikes, the struggle against exploitation became occasions in which the priest confronted the communist movement and discovered it in all its organizational and messianic political force. We should not forget that the years after the Second World War in Europe were characterized by the epochal struggle between the two opposing blocs, which assumed the form of a real clash of civilizations between the democratic West (with which the church sided) and the communist East. It was a bitter struggle that involved social life and the church in all its dimensions. The suburbs, with all their poverty, represented a reserve of votes for the left; this was the *banlieue rouge* (red margin) of Paris. On the other hand, with Pius XII as pope, the church called upon Catholics to see the electoral defeat as an option for civilization and liberty. No compromise was allowed. You were either with the church or you collaborated with its enemies, those who persecuted Christianity in communist countries. In 1949, Pius XII issued the *Decree against Communism,* which excommunicated all those who deliberately propagated Marxist ideology.

Was the cause of the struggle by the marginalized against the cause of the church and the faith? How was it possible for priests sent out on mission to support both the church and the working class? How was it possible to be both a priest, remaining obedient to the church, and at the same time a worker living a working-class life in the poor suburbs? And when the church opposed communism, wasn't it against the liberation of the marginalized? These were the questions that beset the worker-priests when in 1954 the order came from Pius XII for priests to give up working in factories. The group split on their response to the pope's order. Most chose "faithfulness" to the working class and refused to give up their work, whereas a minority submitted. Within the Paris Mission, André Depierre submitted to the directive from Rome, though continuing his activity in Montreuil. But many regarded it as impossible to give up their work; they considered that to be an abandonment—even a betrayal—of the working class. They regarded what they were doing as vital. So they did not submit. Among these were Emile Poulat (who, however, did not work in a factory). He began collecting the documents of the worker-priests and later became their historian. He was convinced that this modest story of the marginalized and their struggles deserved to be told and remembered, because it had an importance beyond its narrow range.

About a Failure: So Many Questions

Following difficulties and failures, the 1954 decision appeared to ratify the "divorce" between the church and the proletariat. It seemed possible only to keep certain bastions of Catholicism, parishes or associations, but impossible to build Christian base communities inculturating the Christian faith into a working-class and marginalized mindset. It seemed impossible to have proletarian communities without separating from the church. So did settling in the poor suburbs and taking on their mindset mean parting from the church?

Basically, the marginal world and the world of the church each followed a different logic. This was the conflict that wracked the lives of the worker-priests, torn between two loyalties. That was the lesson drawn by observers of the brief but intense episode, by those who sympathized with the missionary adventure, those who observed the events from a political viewpoint, but also by those who noted how the life of a priest could not adapt to the ways of such a marginalized world. People's opinion of who was to blame differed according to the viewpoint from which they were judging: the hierarchy, Rome, the communist movement, the naiveté of the worker-priests, or the audacity of Cardinal Suhard. Perhaps, however, rather than being the fault of one side or the other, it was the realization that there was a long history of distance between the church, on the one hand, and the working-class, marginal world on the other.

So, as we have said, the worker-priests suffered a clash of two loyalties that seemed incompatible. The marginal world of the poor suburbs, with its dramas but also with its messianic logic of liberation (embodied in the socialist movement opposed to the Catholic world and its organizations), seemed to attract those priests, drawing them far from their roots, their priestly identity, their loyalty to the church, and their own environment. In order to enter the working-class world, of course, it was necessary to go out from the ecclesiastical world and its ways, but was it also necessary to deny any attachment to the church, which had its own explicit historical forms, especially for priests? Was it necessary to adopt the political viewpoint of the working class? Was the church so distant from the marginalized world, so anchored in the ways of bourgeois society, that it could not penetrate that other world?

The brief story of the worker-priests is a big story, because it brings up again a series of questions about twentieth-century Christianity: the relationship between the city church and the margins or poor suburbs, between mission and parish, between belonging to the church and taking part in the socialist movement and revolutionary struggles. These are ongoing questions after Vatican II in Europe but also in Latin America. It is no longer a question of worker-priests but of so many experiences of engagement in liberation struggles by Christians. There is also the problem of the relationship of Christians with Marxism, which became the ideology of the liberation struggle in a large part of the marginalized world. These are problems that seem to have receded after 1989 and the crisis of ideologies, but in the decades after the Second World War and Vatican II they were crucial for those Christians who were in solidarity and wanted to work with the marginalized. Did a passion for the marginalized inevitably involve political activity and ideology?

In a world like the Paris *banlieue* we find many dramatic aspects of twentieth-century history: poverty, exploitation, inhumane working conditions, terrible housing, the desire for liberation. But there was also resignation to a lot that people were unable to change. In addition, there was the marginalization of women, lack of schooling for children, and child labor. The fundamental intuition of the worker-priests was that it is necessary to share in this reality in all its aspects and to make the church grow anew from within the marginalized world. The story does not emanate from the center and reach the margins in a straight line. In its two-thousand-year-old history Christianity has sometimes moved outward from the margins; in fact, it first grew in the margins. The failure of the worker-priests in the mid-1950s shows what shallow roots Christianity has in the marginalized worlds. It also shows—and this is something that needs to be reflected on—how the church's territorial organization (so like the politico-administrative organization of States) no longer corresponds with reality and does not capture it.

A Testing Place for the Centrality of Christianity

For the generation that came of age in the aftermath of the Second World War the margins represented a great human and religious challenge. It was to that territory that the missionary thrust of the worker-priests was directed. Quite a few of them had shared the experience of forced labor in Germany during the German occupation of France: the priests who were sent with the French workers to work with them and give them pastoral care.

More than three hundred French priests and many seminarians chose to share clandestinely in the forced labor of the workers and experienced the life of the camps. In his diary as a priest and worker in Nazi Germany, Henri Perrin tells the story of another priest who had this to say about his mission among the workers forced to work in the German camps. "I came out of simple solidarity with the French working class."[14] Perrin himself was briefly interned in a concentration camp before being sent back to France. He noted:

> If the Lord were to pitch his tent among us again, I believe he would come to find our shop-floors and our camps. And he would end up not on a cross but in a concentration camp.[15]

The camp is the most extreme margin. In the typical concentration camp conditions of being emptied out and relegated, so to speak, to the outskirts of life, Father Perrin sees the presence of Jesus, recognizes him in the prisoners, and regards him as a true friend of the human margins. The margins are not just in the cities, the proletarian suburbs, places of poverty and exploitation, as we have described. During the war and in totalitarian regimes there were margins that were even more extreme. Geneviève de Gaulle-Anthonioz, General de Gaulle's niece, who was very active in social work in France in the aftermath of the Second World War, was deported by the Germans to the Ravensbrück Nazi camp. Here, among other things, she was the companion of the Russian nun Mother Maria Skobtsova, who had been arrested in Paris for hiding some Jews in her house. After the war, when she became acquainted with the Parisian slums, she clearly felt that she was reexperiencing the world of the concentration camp she had experienced during her detention. She writes: "When I entered that great *bidonville* [slum] for the first time, at the end of a muddy road, with no light, I thought of the camp, that other camp, Ravensbrück."[16]

This comparison of the conditions on the extreme margins with the concentration camp, which Geneviève de Gaulle instinctively made, was not fictitious or rhetorical. Of course the situations were different, but there was a likeness, that of exclusion from life, although on different levels. The generation that knew the horror of the camps, the drama of the Shoah, has a deep and tragic sense of life. It knows what extreme exclusion from the human community means. That generation gained a profound capacity to grasp the humiliation of human dignity.

The camps and the gulags are the extreme margins of the human. Many people wondered what it meant to believe, love, and pray in the Nazi camps, questioning what remained of humanity in the midst of such conditions. The same questions arose in the Soviet gulags. We read about Alexander Solzhenitzyn, who experienced the dehumanization process of the gulag system yet found an inner strength to resist through his awareness, faith, and literary vocation. He writes:

> Now I believe in myself and my strength to survive everything. . . . I have learned through personal experience that someone's external life circumstances not only do not exhaust but do not even define or constitute what is essential in their life.[17]

However, sometimes these dramatic experiences break people's lives. If they manage to survive, they remain deeply scarred by what they have endured. We must not forget that during the twentieth century this concentration camp/gulag extreme margin represented a real hell.

Nonetheless, even in this dramatic margin there was prayer and faith. That is the story of Barracks 10 in Dachau, where not only Catholic priests but also clergy from other Christian denominations were detained. It was an experience of prayer, meeting, and ecumenism, as we hear from the testimony of Giuseppe Girotti, who had been arrested and deported for helping the Jews. Girotti lost his life at Dachau. However, in that hell he glimpsed an ecumenical future for the church and looked toward other Christians with hope and expectation. That was very different from the typical, negative church perspective in those years. It was an ecumenism of pain and martyrdom in extreme conditions, whereby unity asserted itself more strongly in the face of historical divisions.

An Italian priest, Roberto Angelo, detained for a long period at Mauthausen, wrote about the presence of priests in the camp in this way:

> Perhaps it was necessary that there should be priests in those places of terror and death. . . . We did not celebrate mass. But in the morning, at roll call, when twenty thousand suffering people in the prison yard began their day of unspeakable pain, we were there to fulfill our office of mediating between God and humanity. That teeming camp was like a great paten, more precious than the golden patens in our churches. . . . Yes, a priest was needed in those places. He had to gather all that infinite pain and present it to God.[18]

The history of Christian martyrdom in the camps and the gulags brings us into contact with a world of horrors, but also a world with faith and humanity that arose from Christian resistance to human evil and destruction. Even on that extreme margin it was possible to remain human, although very often men and women were destroyed. Albania was the first communist State to proclaim a ban on all religious practice in 1967. Gjovalin Zezaj, a young Albanian from Scutari, wrote a memoir of his long imprisonment. He recalled the figure of a prisoner who had been destroyed by torture: "A prisoner came in, supported under his arms. He seemed to have been severely tortured because he could not stand alone and I heard him say between his teeth: 'It's real hell here.'"[19]

The communist concentration camp system was part of a plan to create a society of equals, in short a paradise, but it became a real hell on earth. Hell exists in history, and some people have experienced it. This is a chapter of life on the margins in which it was not possible to organize any formal religious presence, but where only the strength of individuals offered human resistance.

Many people were scarred by this era. The dramatic experiences of a generation that had known—whether intimately or from a distance—the marginalization of the concentration camps, encouraged the Christian impetus toward the margins. This is a subject that needs further study. But it shows how a generation with experience of extreme pain has been able to feel more strongly the scandal of marginalization. As we said, quite a few of the worker-priests had experienced, in one way or another, the painful events of the Second World War. Although he had no personal experience of the camps, Pope John Paul II had been very closely aware of the drama of war in Poland and was convinced that his generation had a

special responsibility to work for peace and the human-
ization of the world.

The Mystique of the Margins

In many ways the twentieth century witnessed an attraction toward the world's margins. Think of Brother
Charles de Foucauld (1858–1916), a hermit and man of
prayer who died alone in the heart of the Sahara. He was
a model for many others who set out on remote paths on
the margins during the twentieth century, to lead a life
of prayer, sharing poverty and friendship. For example,
there were the two religious communities linked to René
Voillaume and Little Sister Magdeleine. And there were
many others who in different ways followed in their
footsteps. For de Foucauld and his followers the Sahara,
the true margin of the world, was where to seek God.

According to René Voillaume, founder of the Little
Brothers of Jesus, Brother Charles's idea of the Christian life was very different from the monastic one,
although it was substantially a life of prayer. For him,
there was no separation from the world, but rather
identification with the life of the poor and marginalized. Such were the Tuareg, among whom de Foucauld
lived and among whom he died in 1916. In a fundamental work for understanding de Foucauld's life and ideas,
Voillaume writes about de Foucauld: "His religious life

tried to reproduce the common life of the poor, the proletariat, and he understood that for this it was necessary to live in small groups." And addressing the Little Brothers who wanted to follow in Brother Charles's footsteps he adds:

> You live among the poor, in order to share more fully in their way of life. You will feel the injustice of their situation in yourselves, in a new way and as if in your own flesh. There will be the insufficient wages and even more the indifference of those who minimize the importance of the problem. In short, it will be the pain of poor families, of children who despair of a future without any opportunities, the anonymous sick people in hospitals and sanatoriums. And in the face of all this, there will be the calm tranquility and self-satisfaction of too great a number of Christians.[20]

However, true to the footsteps of Charles de Foucauld, the Little Brothers and Little Sisters did not become involved in political or trade-union struggles. They immersed themselves in sharing the conditions of the marginalized, becoming vulnerable, like them. There is a link between life on the working-class margins, that of the poor in many parts of the world, and the conditions of the desert, where de Foucauld died.

The desert is not just the Sahara (which nevertheless remains an important reference point for the Little Sisters and Little Brothers), but also the city margins and the lands of the poor and houses of the excluded all over the world. There is a mystique of the desert that is also lived on the human margins:

> The "desert" and "Nazareth," the one and the other lived together without compromise, in total charity, for God and human beings, these are the two elements that make up the richness of our life and make us love it. It would be a misunderstanding of the life of the Little Brothers to reduce it to the apparent human difficulty of their work. If a contemplative life gives the Little Brothers the strength to create a unity between their living for God and their work, that is because of the "desert." Here lies the great lesson of Brother Charles of Jesus.[21]

Voillaume concludes (while he was writing he was also aware of the crisis caused by the end of the worker-priests in 1954):

> We can be very daring when we mix among people, because we come from the desert and go back

there. But these two lives are not contradictory or
alternative. They are united by the same state of
mind of poverty, eucharistic life, and a single desire
to save souls through the constant intercession of
solitary prayer.[22]

Voillaume experienced the lacerating disappointment
of the end of the worker-priests and confrontation with
class struggle. All this was discussed among the Little
Brothers, but he stressed the primacy of universal love,
lived on the margins as opposed to within the social
struggle, even when motivated by just aims. In 1950,
he wrote, "You must lovingly seek in everyone not that
which divides but that which unites."[23]

The proletarian world is the second desert after
de Foucauld's Sahara. And along these lines the Little
Brothers and the Little Sisters discover many others,
extending their fellowship to many parts of the world,
the places where the poor live, the human and social
margins, the lands of the marginalized. For Little Sister
Magdeleine, in 1947, this became a call to universality.
"We are far from our little closed circle of France where
it is easy to think you are the center of everything." In her
own way Magdeleine works out a spiritual geopolitics of
the margins, seeking the most excluded on the planet
among whom to set up her sisterhood. "Look at the map

of the world," she writes in 1950. "Above all, look at the number of unhappy people in the world who are calling out to us: the prisoners, the deported, the peddlers, the dishwashers."[24]

The adventure of the Little Sisters and the Little Brothers involves a utopia, a different way of being Christian in the world, which in so many places has become a human desert: "We need to build something new; something new that is ancient, according to the genuine Christianity of Christ's first disciples. We must take up the gospel again word for word. It is so painful to see that it has been forgotten."[25] At the end of his last book Father Voillaume suggests a way to renew Christianity. His first suggestion is simple: very little that is new and peacemaking can be done in the church without being in communion with the church. That is his experience, endured amid many difficulties. He adds that the Christian does not have readymade solutions for the difficult problems of the modern world but knows that prayer is the right and human way to look to the future. And: "Perhaps we are entering a period in the history of the human race which will be a time of pity for our inability to find solutions to our problems. It will be more necessary than ever to offer ourselves in intercession."[26] For Voillaume, the places for intercession are, above all, not monasteries but on the margins.

Women on the Margins

In many societies in the twentieth and twenty-first centuries, women are marginalized from the world that counts, where the real power lies. However, in the church it is often women who travel to the furthest worlds for the sake of humanity and the gospel. There is the significant example of the option for the poor suburbs made by Little Sister Magdeleine, the founder of the Little Sisters of Jesus in the spirit of Charles de Foucauld. She shared the lives of the lowest and poorest in an existence centered on prayer. From the mid-1940s the founder and her sisters lived in the poor suburbs in a "feminine" way. In 1942, she wrote: "Before being nuns, be Christians. Have the simply human virtues of hospitality and charity to the highest degree. And only after that add the virtues of the religious life."[27]

The women did not set up convents but lived in poor, simple houses among the people, in tents with the Tuaregs, or in caravans with the Gypsies, sharing the lives and conditions of all as Christian women. The Little Sisters were not protected by the rhythms and walls of religious life. For them, humanity was decisive: first and foremost they were to be Christian human beings, not nuns. That was their constant teaching. In the midst of people, often the poor, the Little Sisters—their founder wished—should always be lit up by a "smiling kindness":

Be ever more hospitable. Let lay visitors leave our
houses with their hearts warmed by your smiling
kindness. Do not look at all severe. You would be
completely on the wrong track if you behaved
harshly, which would be quite out of place for
us. On the roads of Galilee Jesus was all smiling,
sweet, and tender.[28]

The founder's first choice was the extreme margin
of France, so to speak: the Sahara desert. Here Brother
Charles de Foucauld lived as a hermit, hoping to gather
a community, only in the end to be killed while he was
still alone. So the story of the Little Sisters of Jesus
begins in the Sahara desert: that was a decisive test.
From the desert, a remote land in Algeria that was going through some very difficult years, these women's
passion grew for other marginal places, because it
seemed easier to understand the world from there.
Magdeleine opened sisterhoods in many countries,
never creating works or buildings, but always setting
her sisters among the poor, as small communities of
women capable of sharing the lives of all without any
missionary or proselytizing aim.

Magdeleine withstood strong pressures from the
ecclesiastical world, which wanted the Little Sisters to
be more protected by convents and behave more like
nuns with a regulated life. She was also asked to take on

the responsibility of schools, dispensaries, or other social works. But although she considered these to be useful, they did not accord with the vocation of the Little Sisters. Her answer was clear: the Little Sisters live on the margins, not in order to lead, organize or build, but to be among poor people. She writes:

> We have only one single aim: to become "one of them," that is, one of the poorest, the class of the lowest, those whom the world despises . . . never on a higher level than them in order to lead them, educate them, or instruct them, but on an equal level, in order to love them and help them, as you would help your own friends, your own brothers and sisters, those who are like you. That is our only way![29]

From the Sahara to the world of the working class, to the forsaken rural districts in France, to North Africa, with the African poor—like the Pygmies—and even to the slums in the great Latin American and Asian cities, Magdeleine wanted to create "centers of sweetness, peace and love" among people through the poor and simple lives of her sisters. Thus, some Little Sisters could be seen roaming with the Gypsies, while others became peasants or workers, at the same time being nuns and nearly always wearing religious habits.

Sisterhoods even grew in the Middle East, a complex world that has experienced the conflict between the Arabs and Israelis after the Second World War and where they were confronted with the world of Islam. The Little Sisters were to create simple places that were friendly, open, and accessible to all. Their way of conversing was through their friendship and lifestyle. Without preaching or proselytizing, the Little Sisters showed that it was possible to be human beings and believers, even in the most forgotten and battle-torn corners of the world. These were women who had moved out of their home environment to live among the poor and to see the world with the eyes of the marginalized.

In 1951, in an Africa still dominated by colonialism, Magdeleine made a journey to Cameroon. This journey moved her deeply, and she wrote some significant pages about her experience. She met the Pygmies, who were discriminated against by the neighboring African populations (who in their turn were discriminated against by the white colonial powers) and conceived the plan to set up a sisterhood among them. With their human warmth and life of comradeship and prayer, the Little Sisters were able to give these people, humiliated by colonialism and despised by other ethnic groups, the message that they were not forsaken. On this human margin, the Little Sisters were a feminine, friendly, and Christian presence. That was the strength of a "weak" witness by these Christian women.

Without criticizing the activities of the missionaries, Little Sister Magdeleine distanced herself from their ways of behaving; she was seeking a new kind of religious life. She saw a "wall" to be knocked down that divided Europe from Africa, Europeans from Africans, a very deep division that was destined to last a long time. She also perceived the distance of the missionary church, with its institutions, from the Africans. She believed that only love would pull down the wall. In colonial Africa the Little Sisters wanted to be an expression of love, and they themselves represented a sisterhood made up of people from different national, ethnic, and cultural backgrounds. Magdeleine saw an imminent change coming on this immense colonial margin. In 1951 she wrote: "My soul is overflowing with the desire for sisterly love between black and white people." That was a dream that began to come true with the sisterhoods in Africa. The Little Sisters' way of life was to stay among the poor and marginalized with a joyful and communicative humanity. But it was not always easy. She writes:

> Be human in order to glorify the Father better. . . .
> The more perfectly and totally human you are, the
> more perfectly and totally you will be able to be a

nun, because your religious perfection will flower
when it is balanced by what it is based on.[30]

Following their founder, the Little Sisters lived among
the most marginalized people, at the same level and with
their poor possessions, without distinguishing themselves
even with the pretext of being religious. They created
a network of fellowship on five continents, formed—I
repeat—by sisters from the most varied national backgrounds, who did not try to exercise influence over
society or the church, but rather to create a human and
gospel presence in society's remote places. "It's pure
madness," wrote the founder, "to send out two by two,
just like that, such young and poorly prepared little
sisters." The Little Sisters opted for the world's margins
while maintaining a strong unity among themselves
throughout their sisterhood.

A Woman in the Marxist City

At about the same time as the creation of the Little
Sisters, a woman chose to live as a Christian on the
banlieue rouge (red margin) of Paris in a working-class
environment. She was Madeleine Delbrêl, who in 1933
settled in Ivry, the Paris suburb where she lived until
her death in 1964. Her life was interwoven with that of
the worker-priests. In fact, Cardinal Suhard appointed

her as a member of the consultative commission at their beginning. Her life was also linked with the Little Sisters, whom she knew and visited.

Madeleine had a strongly original character, marked by her specifically feminine approach, her gospel insight, and her sympathy with the environment in which she lived. She describes a meeting in a social center: "On the wall there is a map of the area. The group immediately splits in two: all the women go to the window, all the men stand in front of the map. It's a small point but it says a lot. The great teaching given by women is life."[31]

A group of women friends shared Madeleine's life in that poor working-class environment, a municipality run by the Communist Party, which was in conflict with the church. Ivry belonged to the red belt round the capital, where social life was strongly influenced by the Party. The clash between the Communists (called *cocos*) and the Catholics (nicknamed the *curés*) was total; there was no intermediate space between them. Madeleine and her companions were not prepared to live only in the parish environment, or to be identified with the area bosses, even if they were Catholic. They did not want to be confined within the logic of this political clash. They intended to meet people in their daily lives. They were moved by the wretched conditions in which the working-class masses and their families lived.

Madeleine and her friends did not want to be parish people, but rather to be open to contact with everyone on the street. They organized a gospel circle, a meeting to read a page of the Gospel relevant to the situation. Madeleine acted as a social helper and agreed to lead the family social services on behalf of the Communist municipality. She felt she had to work to change the difficult situation of many people in Ivry. She collaborated with the institutions, at that time run by the Party, and knew the Communists well. This is how she described the world on the margins, as she came across it every day:

> Women despondent at an imminent birth or dying at the hands of women who procured improvised abortions. . . . Weak, divided parents. Houses built of make-shift materials. Children with no childhood. Abandoned old people surviving with their compulsory social card. And as well, the desolation of the neglected lodgings: impersonal furnished rooms, classic slums with unmade bed and sticky oilskin tablecloth.[32]

Madeleine's and her companions' social activities were conducted in a family spirit and an attitude, as she wrote, of "universal brothers and sisters." They didn't undertake bureaucratic or repressive inspections. People in need were not regarded as cases but as friends of this community of women. Being close to marginalized people and the dramas in their actual lives was the vocation of Madeleine and her companions. They did not feel different from the people, even though they were witnesses to the gospel message. They believed that all Christians were missionaries: "A crowded desert. To plunge into the crowd as into white sand."[33] Indeed, Ivry seemed to Madeleine like a new desert of life and solidarity, in which hundreds of thousands of people lived in inhuman conditions and without any comfort. The link between the biblical theme of the desert and the margins is recurrent in so many Christian experiences in the twentieth century.

The need, Madeleine believed, was to be among the people without believing you belonged to a world apart (whether that of the parish or the religious community), dressing like them, and living side by side with them. In 1937 Madeleine wrote:

> We, the ordinary people of the street, believe with all our might that this street, this world in which God has set us, is our place of holiness. To find a fulfilling occupation in love, we do not distinguish between prayer and action. For us prayer is action and action is a prayer.[34]

These women's activities were not aimed at proselytizing or at countering Communist propaganda, but at a life

centered on "kind, simple, infectious charity" in contact
with all. Thus, a stream of love flows through the world
in which people live, neither watched nor judged from
the outside. Madeleine regarded the worker-priests
with sympathy: "It is vital that the greatest possible
number of priests should be a genuine meeting point
between the world and God," she wrote in 1950.[35] In
fact, a new social reality, the proletariat, was taking
shape, and it was necessary for the church to know and
understand it: "Knowledge of this new land is one of
the great Christian concerns of our time. It is because
of this great concern that so many people—both priests
and laity—have plunged into environments previously
unknown to them."[36]

This marginal world was a place where the Communist Party had organized a movement of self-liberation.
Madeleine lived within the Communist world and, in
1957, she described her experiences of it.[37] Understanding the significance of the Communist reality from
the inside, Madeleine was convinced that Christianity
should not give up communicating the gospel and that
Christians should meet Communists on human terms
and work together, respecting how much there was that
was positive in their activities. This was the point Madeleine reached after long experience during which she
met and quarreled with the Communists, attracted by

their dedication but not sharing their ideology. In 1961, on the eve of the Second Vatican Council, she declared:

> The church speaks of communism on the basis of its universal principles and universal action. In Ivry if we distance ourselves from everything the Communists do, we distance ourselves from public life itself, because they have it all in hand. The surprising thing is that for Christians there is only one important thing to do, and that is to stand face to face with the Communist next door, on his landing, in his factory or in his office, and that is exactly what the gospel asks us to do: to stand face to face with anybody. And that takes us a long way![38]

The world of the red margins of Paris was not empty of opportunities for social and political presence. It was not a place lacking ideas for action and a reading of the situation. Rather, it seemed that Christians were marginalized and pushed into the position of a besieged minority or confined to restricted circuits. The reality of the Marxist world and Communist militancy tended to occupy the political scene and social life itself. That was life as it was in Ivry and the Paris red belt. However, Madeleine did not accept either the marginalization or the ideological prejudice. It was necessary to stand

face to face with Communists as women and men and
meet them on a human level. Living in Ivry showed "an
unexpected face of hope: provocation by Marxism to a
vocation for God." She writes:

> Without wanting or expecting to, Marxism forces
> Christians to a sharp realization of the incompa-
> rable importance of God, to a self-development
> which moves on from Marxism to confront the
> greatest of human questions: does God exist?[39]

Madeleine Delbrêl measured herself against the Communists in human contact and daily meetings. For all
its human contradictions, to her the movement itself
looked different from how it might appear from the
perspective of the center, either that of the church or
of political institutions. Above all, she was aware of a
challenge or, as she preferred to say, a "call" to a Christian
maturity and a personal adherence to the gospel. In short,
in Madeleine's Delbrêl's thinking there is a theology of the
other that is measured by meeting other people and understanding their situation. That is something that cannot
be forgotten, even today, so many years later, when the
poor suburbs have undergone a profound transformation.
(Think of Paris where a decisive factor is the presence of
Muslims). According to Madeleine, Christians should ask:
who is the other? And what kind of response does that

question provoke, if Christians are not to remain shut up in ghettos and minority enclaves? Often, not meeting the other deprives Christians of that fundamental "call" which makes them aware of their actual mission.

What strikes us in the story of Madeleine Delbrêl and her writings, so imbued with human experience and practical observation of the world in which she lived, is the gospel passion for the margins, with all its poverty, wretchedness, and contradictions. And it was a passion felt from a position of social minority, but also from constant contact with insoluble problems. That attitude is the expression of a great missionary feeling, so to speak, experienced by a good number of men and women in the twentieth century, not only in the global South, in other civilizations and cultures, but in cities of Europe.

Sant'Egidio: The Poor Suburbs and the City

The Second Vatican Council encouraged the impulse to go out from ecclesiastical institutions and also from one's own environment. The story—or rather, stories—of this outgoing are many and complex. However, they are concerned with a strong drive, a passion, which was also generational, arising from the spirit of the council and spreading in many different ways throughout all the latitudes of the church. The council stirred a passion for the margins. Many of these stories remain undiscovered.

On a personal note, I cannot fail to mention the story of the Sant'Egidio Community, at first in Rome and then in the wider world. The community arose on the margins of Rome. This was the world of the so-called Roman *borgate*—poor suburbs—where, from the fascist years, the capital's most marginalized groups had congregated. After the Second World War constant immigration from the south of Italy had enlarged the margins of Rome, while the city changed its appearance. In those years slums—*borghetti* and actual shanty towns—arose that, in some ways, made Rome like a third-world city:

> It was a sorry procession of humanity, rather different from the images propagated by the crime news of prostitutes, thieves, and scoundrels. Of course, there were also these, but they were overwhelmed by the stubborn, silent black figures of peasants from Calabria, Abruzzi and Sicily, each group with its own way of speaking and the smell of its own land.[40]

During the 1960s and 1970s, a great distance was clearly to be seen between the "regular" city and the Rome of the slums and poor suburbs. The people living in slums were estimated to be between 30,000 and 100,000, while the population of the poor suburbs hovered around 600,000. This world was also joined by those evicted from the city center (driven out during the fascist period in order to build an "imperial" city), impoverished Romans side by side with all sorts of people from everywhere. There were also the immigrants from the south of Italy, who constantly flowed into Rome: people living in poverty, doing casual jobs, and often living in unfit accommodations. It was from here that the Roman building trade, the real business of the capital, got its laborers, offering work that was often precarious.

The church was generally distant from this environment, despite some significant presences, often of a charitable kind. At most, there was a client relationship between these people and the church institutions, from whom they could get some help, a way of managing to get by, typical of the Roman marginalized. The people from the slums were usually absent from the parish Sunday mass. Although the parish may have been geographically close to those slums, it was not their world. They did not feel at home in a Catholic environment, even though quite a few of them kept up some form of religious piety. There were many factors in play: a traditional detachment from the church (sometimes imbued with a new or ancient anticlericalism), a distance from the institution they had grown up with when they left their lands, and a communication failure between the forms of parish life and "slum" culture.

There was popular religiosity among the marginalized, but each group kept to its own local traditions and did not integrate with the religious world of Rome. Moreover, at least until 1974, when the church of Rome promoted a great conference on the ills of the city, these poor worlds were not at the heart of the church's activity, even though there were a number of significant institutions and initiatives.

It was mainly the Italian Communist Party, with its base groups, that took up the desire of the marginalized for liberation and a better life. And indeed, the Party won the 1975 municipal elections. In Rome this was unprecedented and, in some ways, devastating for the Catholics, who had always ruled the city in the postwar period. After 1968, the Roman margins were inundated with committees and associations, arising with the leftwing surge, even beyond the Communist Party: they promoted social and political activities and self-organization.

After Vatican II, in a Christian world stirred by the council, the Sant'Egidio Community—formed in 1968 by students at a high school in the center of Rome—turned its attention to the poor suburbs. It began solidarity work, particularly with children (who often did not attend compulsory school), the old, and the poorest. At that time they were mainly young people, members of a community in its early stages, who went into the world of the marginalized, wanting to share their lives in solidarity. With a previously unimagined human closeness, they created new links with marginal social groups and aroused a desire for liberation among the poorest.

For Sant'Egidio, the people on the margins were the poor, whom they set at the center of Christian life. It was necessary to create a different church, one in which the poor felt at home, neither marginalized, as they were in the lives of many parishes, nor merely clients of charitable institutions. Didn't that mean creating a parallel option to the local church or parish? The community felt painfully the distance between the marginal world and the Christian reality in Rome, especially the lack of a living witness to the gospel to give hope to those whose lives were often hard, and to engage with their widespread religiosity. The diocesan institutions were a parallel world to this one. The starting point had to be the demand for the gospel in these poor suburbs. From that, a religious and communal journey could begin within that world, rooted in it; it would not be concerned about bringing those who were distant from them back into the ecclesiastical institutions.

Over the years Sant'Egidio's work grew within the worlds of the marginalized, the city's poor suburbs and *borgate*, a series of Christian communities where the poor felt at home and the program of "good news to the poor" (Luke 4:18), announced by Jesus in the synagogue at Nazareth, began to be put into practice. The meeting places were often very humble; spaces were found under buildings or in improvised venues where people lived and led their daily lives. Here, reading the Gospel, liturgy, and prayer were interwoven with solidarity, personal friendship, and new forms of contact among the marginalized people. It was a little "story" that seemed almost irrelevant, but from which something important emerged: the fruitfulness of the gospel read and lived on the margins.

In these communities there were many women, who bore the brunt of daily difficulties and family life. They were the most marginalized, suffering the disadvantaged position of women and heavy dependency on men. The drama of clandestine abortions often affected their lives and health. They were also victims of violence, frequent and recurrent, barely hidden. In the 1960s the condition of women in Rome was very hard, with high rates of illiteracy. Often women lived in a state of de facto segregation in the *borgate*, much more so than men. Their horizon was the suburb, the small local area, out of circulation, with the city far away. Becoming a domestic servant was often the only way of getting out of this world and gaining economic independence. But in the communities that arose in these poor suburbs the women became protagonists even before the men, and beyond the confines of their local area. They became witnesses to a message of how to live and communicate in their own environment.

For men, apart from laboring in the building trade, jobs were mostly precarious. There was a short path from being marginalized to being criminal, and there were many who went that way, quite often ending up in prison. Adults and old people often carried with them the memory of painful or difficult histories they had suffered, poverty in the past, emigration, two wars, fascism. These people—women, men, children and old people—were the ones addressed by the Sant'Egidio Community in the poor suburbs. A community of the marginalized arose who felt they had found a "center" in the gospel and hope in their lives.

A sense of fellowship grew among these people in their individual and communal reading of the word of God. Their scant education did not prevent their familiarity with the sacred text. It took time for these communal activities, which grew out of a dream of the gospel, to connect with other more or less institutional forms of the church's presence.

In 1987 a short book, *Vangelo in periferia* [Gospel on the margins], gathered a series of reflections on the Bible, which arose from the lives of the communities over the years. In his preface Cardinal Martini of Milan observed that the world of the marginalized had imbued the texts and comments, which were not "the result of deskwork":

The attention of the people of the Roman *borgate* also explains the recurrence of themes, images, and sufferings typical of that world: the winter cold for those who find it hard to protect themselves in damp houses, loneliness, sickness, the situation of women.[41]

Before becoming archbishop of Milan, Martini had been in Rome, one of the commentators on the gospel in these *borgata* communities with Sant'Egidio, sharing some moments of their life and Bible study in these marginalized environments. He celebrated mass every Sunday in a former pizzeria, which had been transformed into a chapel and meeting place in the Alessandrina *borgata*.

He himself told this story, recalling also how, feeling he had reached the limit of university teaching and biblical studies, he had sought places in the city where the gospel was lived. Thus he met with the Sant'Egidio Community and shared in the life of its marginal communities. According to his experience, "the original inspiration . . . was about prayer, scripture, the poor, community, society." He writes:

At the beginning of the 1960s I was walking one afternoon along the street of Trastevere. I was reflecting on a certain split that existed in the immediate aftermath of the council, between those who focused on commitment to the poor, to transform society, and those who focused totally on spirituality and prayer. And I said to myself: there must be some practical way of reconciling the two, a practical way of uniting in our lives the sense of the primacy of God, the primacy of the Word and prayer, and a vitally urgent, practical, effective love for the poor, contact with people, those who are the most forsaken. . . . It was then [speaking about Sant'Egidio] that I began to grasp, to appreciate this lived-out synthesis between the primacy of God, prayer and hearing the Word: taking God's Word seriously and devoting yourself effectively and in a practical way to the poor.[42]

Commenting on *Vangelo in periferia* and the Sant'Egidio experience in the poor suburbs, Bishop Pietro Rossano, a meticulous biblical scholar and man of humanistic culture, noted the silhouettes of "the women and children, these people from the South, the unemployed, people living in cardboard or tin houses, just to sleep in." These people did not seem that far from the people in the Gospels: the crippled woman, the epileptic boy, the woman taken in adultery. They were the poor of the Roman *borgate,* "but also of the great marginal areas of cities everywhere." And here Rossano asked the question about the message carried by the presence of Sant'Egidio in the poor suburbs: "What does the gospel bring to these people? Why do they listen to it?" He continues:

The gospel does not bring employment, does not bring medicine, does not bring food, does not even bring the morality of the wise, that is sometimes alien to Christians. Neither does it bring the condemnation which indignant moralists often hurl. Nor does the gospel bring revolution and class hatred.[43]

Rossano continued by asking, What does the gospel bring to marginalized people, beset by so many problems of daily life? He answered: "The gospel is . . . a proclamation and also an energy; it is a ray of light and hope, it is company and affection, transmitted individually and through the community." That is a declaration that could be shared by many who lived through this history. Rossano concluded by asking what the gospel added to the lives of the marginalized: "It is an energy that is communicated through the mysterious, fragile interpersonal relations of affection and sharing that one person brings to another."[44]

This is the story of the Sant'Egidio Community in the poor suburbs of Rome and other cities, a network of fellowship founded on the gospel. The community developed actions in solidarity with people in difficulties, the poor, the loneliest, the disabled, the old (average life expectancy has increased but has not been accompanied by an increase in the quality of life, so that the final years of life become very painful for the poor). In this respect, even in the world of the marginalized, the realization has grown that no one is ever too poor to help a poor person. The following was written at Sant'Egidio at that period:

> The basic gospel message of liberation seems to me to be that it gives back to all the dignity of being men and women, children of God, brothers and sisters, disciples. The liberation message, put simply but with conviction, is that life can change.[45]

Because I was personally involved in these events, I have generally preferred to quote witnesses to illustrate this story. However, over the years I have realized how, through listening to the word of God, there has been a growth in "a spirituality of men and women of the city, which we spoke about then and now as if it were a desert where the search for God was not impossible. The Book was not eternally sealed for anyone."[46] That is how I wrote then. The poor suburbs could be inhabited by Christian communities of marginalized people. It was possible to live the gospel in this world, even though not by means of institutional forms. Cardinal Ugo Poletti, vicar of Rome from 1973, who was very attentive to the poor suburbs, understood the value of these forms of presence and defended them against an ecclesiastical mentality that tried to reduce everything to institutional geometry. He wrote in 1988:

> I have seen your community growing here in Rome—at first almost timidly in schools, in the *borgate,* then little by little on the city's large marginal outskirts… I am happy to have always been close to you, happy for myself and for our dear diocese which finds in you a witness to its universal mission.[47]

This is what I wrote on the occasion of an anniversary of the Community in the poor area of Primavalle in Rome, a marginal district of the city but significant in terms of the gospel:

> Above all, an idea, a dream, has come true and become a reality: that all could receive the gospel. Neither age, nor social situation, nor difficulties in life could prevent the reception of the gospel; no

one is ever so deaf or has such a difficult life that he or she can't receive the gospel. Here we have realized the meaning of the gospel in the poor suburbs: the gospel for everyone.[48]

Conclusion

Gospel on the Margins

Human conditions changed rapidly in the twentieth century. At the beginning of the century only a tenth of the world's inhabitants lived in cities, particularly in North America and Europe. But it is predicted that by 2030 nearly 60 percent of the world's population will be urban. The planet has now become urbanized. During the last century there was a major change that reversed the relationship between city and country. With the progress of globalization, in 2007, for the first time in human history, the inhabitants of cities outnumbered those living in rural areas. But all that happened in a very particular way: a large part of city populations now live on the margins. Third-world cities are still divided between center and margin in the contemporary socioeconomic world, not only in the urban centers but in whole countries.

The margins, with agglomerations that crowd around cities, are a major mark of the contemporary world. Indeed, the global urbanization process causes a phenomenon characteristic of the contemporary city: so-called *slumification*. In 2003, 71 percent of the population of sub-Saharan Africa lived in slums. In Africa, being marginalized is the most widespread urban living condition. At a world level, slum dwellers make up 31.6 percent of the population. That is an enormous number of people. It is a world that has no voice but receives constant messages from the center (the media), attracting them to a standard of living that is beyond their reach. The marginalized are the excluded, yet they are in continual contact with an unattainable lifestyle.

The practical problems created by the rapid changes in the living conditions of the world population are many and varied. There are problems with the provision of food, with decreasing our polluted water resources, with urban transport (inadequate or very poor in some cities), and the obvious but dramatic difficulties of work. The human and social reality of the twenty-first-century city is very different from the twentieth-century city. Though the great proletarian (marginalized) masses in the twentieth-century city were often in a dialectical or confrontational relationship with the "center" through political and trade union struggle, despite this conflict they remained within a common horizon. Through the clash and politicization of the aspirations of the margins, an interconnected process was created between the different parts of society.

It is very different today. The margins are much more integrated than in the last century in terms of communications and networks. Socially and politically, however, they are detached. Here the social networks are often weak or absent. Control over marginal urban spaces is complex and difficult, so that vast areas—especially in the megalopolises—end up under the sway of national or even international crime cartels.

This is a worrying (and growing) characteristic of our time: the relation between the margins and the mafias and crime networks, which are also networks of control and "social assistance." The global city is often a place where violence intensifies. We have only to think of some Mexican cities under the control of drug traffickers, or youth gangs in Central America, like the *maras* of El Salvador and Honduras. Significantly, in just over ten years El Salvador has passed from a war between the State and the guerrillas (with an ideology), which ended in the 1990s, to a democracy in which juvenile mafias control the margins, threaten the cities, and enlist a growing part of the younger generation. At the beginning of the 1990s Hans Magnus Enzensberger noted:

On the one hand there are areas protected by security services and, on the other, there are slums and urban ghettoes. In the abandoned districts the

public offices, police patrols and courts no longer
have any power. Violence eludes all control.[1]

Twenty-first-century cities, particularly the megalopolises, share a decreasing common lot. While part
of the city is absorbed into the global flux and directed
towards internationalization, another part remains on
the margins outside the integration circuits, or even
sinks into a state of isolation. These are the abandoned
districts where people often live their whole lives, and
where, perhaps, their children will lead the same lives as
their parents. The megalopolises are structured in such
a way that much of the inhabited space becomes a place
of exclusion, often in the conditions described above.
The megalopolises constantly produce urban margins
and marginalized human beings. Often, especially in the
global South, the State and its institutions give up any
real control over these areas. They become a lost world
in which human and social dramas are interwoven with
criminal networks and endemic rebellion within a culture of survival.

The twenty-first-century margins challenge the
churches; they are a "call," as Madeleine Delbrêl would
still say today. The call came in the last century, and
now it is particularly urgent. Perhaps today the Catholic
Church is less attentive. It does not feel challenged by
Marxist ideology and the competing forces inspired by

it. It has fewer personnel to deal with this situation, even though—as Pope Francis shows—it cannot be said that there is not an acute awareness of the challenge posed by the marginalized worlds. Are these worlds lost to the church and to Christianity?

Under the impulse of Pope Francis, Christianity has the capacity to understand the twenty-first-century human and urban conditions in a new way. Of course, this process demands profound changes. It is no longer possible to tackle it by the territorial mapping typical of former times, which was strongly influenced by a rural world that divided the terrain into predefined areas. The very idea of a territory as the exclusive habitat of a person is now questionable because of human mobility and transport, as well as Internet communication. The pastoral system—often based on pastoral plans and a network of responsibilities—has become inadequate. The Catholic Church still has a territorial vision, divided into dioceses and parishes.

With the growth of cities it has been realized that dioceses have become too big. To give two examples, huge cities like São Paulo and Paris have been subdivided into a number of dioceses. Areas that have become too big are carved up. That subdivision of large dioceses, now consolidated over some decades, has not always been done successfully; more important, it is not innovative. It corresponds to the idea of a church still ruled from the center, but needing more human and less enormous areas. In fact, the real problem is not to reduce the large dioceses into smaller subdivisions, but for the church to be reborn on the margins, to make room for Christian communities and experiences that arise there. The geo-spatial vision on which so much pastoral work has been based has become inadequate. It is not a question of abolishing the center, or the communion between these two realities, but of encouraging a movement that comes from the margins and relates to Christian life there.

After Vatican II, with the renewal of ecclesiology, there was strong emphasis on the local church, but it was a renewal that only went halfway. The local church itself often has a centralized vision that leaves no room for the margins. It is not enough to divide up the dioceses and bring the center nearer to the mar-gins (sometimes this has led to a decrease in human resources and reduced mobility). What is needed is to create new Christian realties on the margins, accept-ing their history and configuration. Not everything can be programmed from the center. And the diversity of Christian experiences in the same territory does not mean competition. The heart of the matter is a Christi-anity that is inserted into the urban culture and reality, especially on the margins.

For Holy Week in 1984 Cardinal Martini, archbishop of Milan, celebrated the Way of the Cross on the streets of the city, not pausing in accordance with the traditional stations, but confronting new urban sufferings: violence, loneliness, drugs, corruption. His comment about that option was that people of the city today are thirsting "for a gospel that is explained to them in a way that affects them and that they can understand. . . . The gospel is read in the city, which is the new horizon where human life with its drama takes place."[2] A gospel read in the city and dealing with its sufferings leads to contact with the margins as a special place for Christian living. And—I repeat—this is a gospel read and lived in a way that comes close to marginalized people.

Speaking to the superior generals of religious communities, Pope Francis made an important statement:

> I am convinced of one thing: the great changes in history were realized when reality was seen not from the center but rather from the periphery. It is a hermeneutical question: reality is understood only if it is looked at from the periphery, and not when our viewpoint is equidistant from everything.[3]

The complexity of the global world, of the megalopolises, cannot be grasped from a hypothetical center, whether ecclesiastical, diocesan, or other. Pope Francis continued:

Truly to understand reality we need to move away
from the central position of calmness and peaceful-
ness and direct ourselves to the peripheral areas.
Being at the periphery helps to see and to understand better, to analyze reality more correctly, to
shun centralism and ideological approaches.[4]

Francis's "hermeneutic key" is not a plan to reform the
church by means of more decentralized structures. In my
opinion, it is a proposal to be received and carried out
by creativity, setting up or continuing initiatives on the
margins and with a view from below. In fact, we need
to ask what it means to live the gospel in such a changed
global urban world or, I would say, in a "civilization" that
is new in so many ways, brought about by globalization.
In order to carry out such an important operation, which
represents a historic transition for twenty-first-century
Christianity, we must move into the margins as an experience of Christian living and a starting point for understanding reality. That is not an ideological position, but
rather rethinking a story that can and must start again
from there and develop a vision in these environments.
In a globalized world we cannot reproduce the church
structure of previous centuries.

In the city the church is divided between an already
existing (and sometimes ancient) organization, based
on territory, and the need to start again with a changed

and mobile human reality. However, it is not the time for pastoral plans or voluntarism. As *Evangelii gaudium* indicates, it is time to start new ways for the church and the gospel, beginning from many different situations. We need to stress the dimension of starting again from the margins.

The church in the city is not so much a well-articulated ecclesiastical area, presided over by pastoral institutions, as a communion of all sorts of ways of living the gospel, through community experiences and human and Christian lives. There must be multiple approaches to that global city. This different understanding must transform the very idea of the parish, which is not so much a pastoral command center of a marked-out territory with a number of Catholics assigned to its care, as a sanctuary to go and pray in, to find a space for silence, to act in solidarity, and to meet as friends. The "sanctuarization" of the parish—a term used in the pastoral theology of Buenos Aires—represents an important change to a Catholic structure based on territory (which still must not neglect its traditional functions).

The parish cannot be the only presence or the one that absorbs the whole of Christian life within a territory. Space needs to be given in Catholicism to the charismatic spirit and to a plurality of Christian ways of living that are not based on an impulse to program and lead everything. The capacity for evangelization shown by the

Protestant charismatic movement represents a significant challenge to the Catholic Church to find new ways, but without getting lost in slavish imitation, which would be completely out of place. It is not a matter of setting up "parallel churches" within Catholicism, but neither should there be an obsession with the idea of controlling everything and enclosing everything within an ecclesiastical geometry. We must understand how the global city requires many different ways to reach the hearts of its people and the heart of the margins. For the Catholic Church, with a scarcity of clergy, the question remains of who will carry out this process of a new beginning for the Christian communities.

The subject of the margins and the global city marks a fundamental step forward from the purely ecclesiastical idea of the church and pastoral work to an idea of a church of people. Of course, this does not mean undervaluing the priestly ministry, just not concentrating all the responsibility for pastoral work upon it (which is what generally happens despite so many speeches against clericalism). The task is to enable people to emerge who in their complexity and entirety are capable of communicating the gospel, living the gospel on the city margins—to give rise to different ways of being Christian, even though they converge in the single great family of the church.

Perhaps we are at the start of an epochal turning point, forced upon us by the history of the twenty-first century. Francis's papacy has had a liberating effect on the existing problems, thereby raising contradictions and questions. If the change is not made, Catholicism will inevitably be left largely outside the world of the margins. Not only will it fail to reach and expand in these environments, but it will exclude itself from them. Even in societies with a Christian tradition, it will end up becoming a minority amid a world of minorities. Rather than being secularized, our time is thick with a fine dust of religiosity, with a whole lexicon of religious words and messages being diffused. But how will the gospel reach this world where religion is nebulized?

The epochal turning point is the transition from an ecclesiastical community to a church of people; its decisive factor is the Christianity that lives on the margins. It is a process that Francis was aware of and began, but which cannot be the product of the will of a single man, regardless of his charismatic character and ecclesial authority. It is the ripening fruit of a renewed gospel passion for the margins and the marginalized. It is a story of enthusiasm for the gospel, rooted in the big cities. Here lie the difficulties of a globalized world with its media, which believes it knows the marginalized but does not want to meet them, or even tries to defend itself from them. How can the passion for the margins be reborn? Nevertheless, despite many signs to the contrary, that enthusiasm has not died, and it remains alive in many human hearts.

Passion for the margins is not only a direction set by Francis's papacy. It is something Christians have already experienced in their history. It is that "exodus" by Christianity from its accustomed confines that has characterized various stages of its history and that today has become a necessity. The passion is also the ability to be challenged by the presence of "others," those who, through their background, are strangers (those of other religions, including Muslims), or separated from Christianity. A missionary Christianity that is capable of a universal impetus (rather than retreating into minority sectarianism) is driven to meet the "other" personally and allows itself to be questioned by that person's otherness.

If we are only at the beginning in certain worlds, if the margins are an alien place for the church, in not a few other worlds there have already been initiatives and work has been undertaken and consolidated. We need to know more about these experiences. We need to let them speak, as they are a page in the life story of the world and the global city. The emergence of this marginal Christianity—no matter how consistent or inconsistent it has been—gives new meaning to the ancient structures, the historical places, and the "sanctuaries" of the church in the city. They can become havens and places of communion for a Christianity of people living in the city, even though they do not always have a voice or are unknown.

Starting again from the margins with the gospel responds to the deep needs of the Christian way in history. It is not a strategy to arrive progressively at the center of society. Rather, it is a decisive step toward the heart of the Christian message. The regeneration of the church and Christian life starts from a passion for the margins and the marginalized, the rediscovery of the joyful task of living and sharing the gospel on the margins.

Notes

1. Jorge Mario Bergoglio, text read to the General Congregation of the Cardinals (March 9, 2013), as quoted in "Vatican—When Cardinal Bergoglio Proposed, 'a Pope Who Would Help the Church to Get Out to the People on the Margins'" (March 14, 2017)J. Daniel, *Ribelli in cerca di una causa: Sommosse nelle periferie francesi* (Milan, 2006), 9.

2. The church of the poor was a major theme of Vatican II.

Chapter 1

1. J. Daniel, *Ribelli in cerca di una causa: Sommosse nelle periferie francesi* (Milan, 2006), 9.

2. H. M. Enzensberger, *Prospettive sulla guerra civile* (Turin, 1994), 11, 41.

3. Ibid. [*Limes* were frontier fortifications that bounded the Roman Empire from the unsubdued Germanic tribes. At the empire's height, the *limes* stretched from the North Sea outlet of the Rhine to near Regensburg (Castra Regina) on the Danube—Trans.]

4. M. Castells, *The Informational City* (Oxford, 1989), 228.

5. Z. Bauman, *Fiducia e paura nella città* (Milan, 2005), 19.

6. W. Bühlmann, *The Coming of the Third Church* (Maryknoll, NY: Orbis Books, 1977), 27.

7. Paul VI, homily at the eucharistic celebration at the end of the Symposium of African Bishops, Kampala (Uganda), July 31, 1969.

8. Philip Jenkins, *The Next Christendom: The Coming of Global Christianity*, 3rd ed. (London: Oxford University Press, 2011 <2002>), 271.

9. Ibid., 275.

10. Pope Francis, meeting with the Bishops of the United States of America, address in the Cathedral of Saint Matthew, Washington DC, September 23, 2015.

11. Pope Francis, interview with Antonio Spadaro, in *A Big Heart Open to God* (San Francisco: HarperOne, 2013), 34.

12. Author's conversation with Cardinal Martini.

13. Claude-Anthime Corbon, *Pourquoi nous vous délaissons: Lettre de l'ouvrier sénateur Corbon au sénateur évêque Dupanloup* (Paris, 1877), in F.-A. Isambert, *Cristianesimo e classe operaia* (Bologna, 1968), 232–58.

14. Ibid.

15. Claude-Anithime Corbon, *Le Secret du peuple de Paris* (Paris: Pagnerre, 1863).

16. Quoted in Christopher Hale, "The World Is Our House!" *Jesuit Educated* (online) (July 30, 2015).

17. Pláticas del p. j. Nadal en el Colegio de Coimbra, SJ, Faculty of Theology, 1945, 69. See also E. Colombo—M. Massimi, In viaggio. Gesuiti italiani candidati alle missioni tra Antica e Nuova Compagnia (Milan, 2014), 28.

Chapter 2

1. A. Spreafico, "Le periferie geografiche e umane nella Scrittura," in *Carità e globalizzazione,* ed. M. Gnavi (Milan, 2014), 85–93.

2. M. Walzer, *Esodo e rivoluzione* (Milan, 2004), 42.

3. Spreafico, "Le periferie geografiche e umane nella Scrittura," 86.

4. Valdo Vinay, *Commenti ai Vangeli* [Comments to the gospels] (Brescia, 1992).

5. J. P. Meier, *A Marginal Jew: Rethinking the Historical Jesus,* 5 vols. (New Haven, CT: Yale University Press, 1991–2016).

6. F. Nietzsche, *The Anti-Christ: Curse on Christianity,* trans. H. L. Mencken (New York: Alfred A. Knopf, 1918), 5, 31, https://en.wikisource.org/wiki/The_Antichrist. Originally published in German as *Der Antichrist: Fluch auf das Christenthum* (1895).

7. See Joseph Ratzinger, *The Meaning of Christian Brotherhood* (San Francisco: Ignatius Press, 1993). Originally published in German in 1960.

8. John Chrysostom, *Homilies on Matthew's Gospel*, Homily 7, in *Nicene and Post-Nicene Fathers, First Series,* vol. 10, ed. Philip Schaff, trans. George Prevost, rev. M. B. Riddle (Buffalo, NY: Christian Literature Publishing Co., 1888), revised and edited for *New Advent* by Kevin Knight, http://www.newadvent.org/fathers/2001.htm.

9. John Chrysostom, *Homilies on Romans,* Homily 15, revised and edited for *New Advent* by Kevin Knight, http://www.newadvent.org/fathers/210215.htm.

10. John Chrysostom, *Homilies on Matthew's Gospel,* Homily 48, alternate translation at newadvent.org/fathers/200148.htm.

11. Saint Ambrose, *On Naboth* 13.56, alternate translation at http://www.hymnsandchants.com/Texts/Sermons/Ambrose/On-Naboth.htm.

12. Olivier Clément, *Riflessioni sull'uomo* (Milan, 1990), 89.

13. Harvey Cox, *The Feast of Fools* (Cambridge, MA: Harvard University Press, 1969).

14. Athanasius, *Life of Saint Anthony* 14, in *Nicene and Post-Nicene Fathers, Second Series,* vol. 4, ed. Philip Schaff and Henry Wace (Buffalo, NY: Christian Literature Publishing Co., 1892). For another English translation, see newadvent.org/fathers/2811.htm.

15. Gregory the Great, *Life and Miracles of Saint Benedict* (Collegeville, MN: Liturgical Press, 1949).

16. Ibid.

17. Benedetto Calati, *Sapienza monastica: Saggi di storia, spiritualità e problemi monastici* (Rome, 1994), 438.

18. Teodoreto, *Storia dei monaci della Siria* (Padua, 1986), 9.

19. Calati, *Sapienza monastica,* 439.

20. Ibid.

21. D. Sorrentino, ed., *Mia sola arte è la fede: Paolino di Nola teologo sapienziale* (Naples, 2000), 64.

Chapter 3

1. Elisabeth Behr-Sigel, *Prière et sainteté dans l'Eglise russe* (Paris, 1950), 94.

2. Elisabeth Behr-Sigel, *Discerner les signes du temps* (Paris, 2002), 38.

3. Archimandrite Spiridon, *Le mie missioni in Siberia* (Turin, 1982), 35–36.

4. Elisabeth Behr-Sigel, "Aleksandr Bucharev: l'ortodossia e il mondo moderno," in *La grande vigilia: Atti del v Convegno ecumenico internazionale di spiritualità russa,* ed. Adalberto Mainardi, 195–210 (Maganano: Comunite Monastica di Bose, 1998), 195–210. Aleksandr Bucharev took the monastic name of Feodor.

5. Behr-Sigel, *Discerner les signes du temps,* 89–90.

6. Evdokimov regarded Father Aleksander Men, who was killed in 1990, perhaps the last victim of the KGB, in the same light as Bucharev (Behr-Sigel, "Aleksandr Bucharev," 195).

7. In Spiridon, *Le mie missioni in Siberia,* 62.

8. Ibid., 78.

9. In ibid., 84.

10. In ibid., 51.

11. Ibid., 53.

12. Ibid., 106.

13. In S. Merlo, *Una vita per gli ultimi: Le missioni dell'archimandrita Spiridon* (Magnano, 2008), 81.

14. Ibid., 184.

15. Lev Gillet, in L. Varaut, *Mat' Marija monaca russa* (Cinisello Balsamo, 2002), 78.

16. Mother Maria, in ibid., 7.

17. Ibid., 8.

18. Ibid.

19. Ibid., 7.

20. Don Giuseppe De Luca, in Romana Guarnieri, *Una singolare amicizia: Ricordando don Giuseppe De Luca* (Genoa, 1998), 110.

21. Ibid.

22. Ibid., 140.

23. In ibid., 151.

24. Don Giuseppe De Luca, in G. Antonazzi, *Don Giuseppe De Luca uomo cristiano e prete (1898–1962)* (Brescia, 1992), 187.

25. Guarnieri, *Una singolare amicizia,* 145.

26. Ennio Francia, *Seminaristi e preti a Roma* (Rome, 1994), 32.

27. Alfredo Calvi [Giuseppe Sandri], *Lettere da Stibbio* (Naples, 1975), 202. Alfredo Calvi was Giuseppe Sandri's pseudonym.

28. Giuseppe Sandri, ed., *San Paolo: Messaggi ai cristiani di Tessalonica e Corinto* (Florence, 2007), 9.

29. Calvi [Sandri], *Lettere da Stibbio*, 203.

30. Giuseppe Sandri, *Attestazione di un piccolo cristiano* (Florence, 1975), 32.

31. [A law allowing divorce in Italy had been passed three years earlier. The referendum was on whether this law should be repealed. Those voting "yes" wanted divorce to become illegal again; those voting "no" wanted it to remain legal.—Trans.]

32. Giuseppe Sandri, ed., *San Paolo: Messaggi ai cristiani di Roma e della Galazia* (Florence, 2009), 9.

33. Giuseppe Sandri, ed., *San Paolo: Messaggi ai cristiani di Filippi, di Colosse, di Efeso, agli Ebrei, a Filemone, a Tito, a Timoteo* (Florence, 2012), 1.

34. Guarnieri, *Una singolare amicizia,* 171.

35. Francesco Marchetti Selvaggiani, in ibid., 153.

36. Giuseppe Sandri, in ibid., 110.

Chapter 4

1. See G. B. Montini, "La carità della Chiesa verso i lontani," in *Discorsi sulla Chiesa* (Milan, 1962), 54.

2. From the vast literature, see Owen Chadwick, *The Secularization of the European Mind in the Nineteenth Century* (Cambridge: Cambridge University Press, 1975).

3. See, for example, Harvey Cox, *The Secular City: Secularization and Urbanization in Theological Perspective* (London: SCM Press, 1965).

4. P. J. Proudhon, *De la Justice dans la révolution et dans l'Eglise* (Paris, 1958), 2:258.

5. René Rémond, "Eglise et monde ouvrier," in *Christianisme et monde ouvrier*, ed. J. Maitron and F. Bedarida (Paris, 1975), 296.

6. In J. P. Guérend, *Cardinal Emmanuel Suhard Archevêque de Paris 1940–1949: Temps de guerre, temps de paix, passion pour la Mission* (Paris, 2011), 243.

7. In ibid., 246–47.

8. Gilbert Cesbron, *Saints in Hell* (New York, 1954).

9. Emile Poulat, *I preti operai* (Brescia, 1967).

10. Guérend, *Cardinal Emmanuel Suhard Archevêque de Paris 1940– 1949*, 245.

11. Karol Wojtyla, quoted in ibid., 272.

12. In M. Barlow, *La foi de Gilbert Cesbron* (Paris, 1989), 54.

13. Marta Margotti, *Preti e operai: La Mission de Paris dal 1943 al 1954* (Turin, 2000), 149.

14. Henri Perrin, *Journal d'un prêtre ouvrier en Allemagne* (Paris, 1945), 305.

15. Henri Perrin, quoted in A. Riccardi, *Il secolo del martirio: I cristiani nel Novecento* (Milan, 2000), 126.

16. Geneviève de Gaulle-Anthonioz, *Le secret de l'espérance* (Paris, 2001), 15–16.

17. Lujdmila Saraskina, *Solženicyn* (Cinisello Balsamo, 2010), 560.

18. Riccardi, *Il secolo del martirio,* 132.

19. Gjovalin Zezaj, *Genocidio medievale nel XX secolo* (Scutari, 2014), 29.

20. For a translation of this work in English, see René Voillaume, *In the Midst of Men, Seeds of the Desert II: The Legacy of Charles de Foucauld* (Fides Publishers, 1966).

21. René Voillaume, *Charles de Foucauld e i suoi discepoli* (Cinisello Balsamo, 2001), 541.

22. Ibid., 556.

23. Ibid.

24. Little Sister Magdeleine, *Il padrone dell'impossibile* (Casale Monferrato, 1994), 222.

25. Ibid.. 201.

26. Voillaume, *Charles de Foucauld e i suoi discepoli,* 556.

27. Piccola Sorella Magdeleine di Gesù, *Dal Sahara al mondo intero* (Rome: Città Nuova, 1983), 105.

28. Ibid., 106.

29. Ibid., 239.

30. Ibid., 364.

31. Ch. Mann, *Madeleine Delbrêl: Una vita senza frontiere* (Turin, 2004), 93– 94.

32. Ibid., 83–84.

33. M. Delbrêl, *Professione assistente sociale* (Milan, 2007).

34. For an alternate English translation, see Madeleine Delbrêl, *We, the Ordinary People of the Street* (Grand Rapids, MI: Eerdmans, 2000).

35. Ibid.

36. Ibid.

37. Madeleine Delbrêl, *Città marxista, terra di missione* [Marxist city, mission country] (Milan, 2015).

38. In Mann, *Madeleine Debrêl,* 203.

39. Delbrêl, *Città marxista*, 131.

40. P. della Seta and G. Berlinguer, *Borgate di Roma* (Rome, 1976), 287.

41. Comunità di Sant'Egidio, *Vangelo in periferia* (Brescia, 1987), 7.

42. C. M. Martini, "Preface," in A. Riccardi, *Sant'Egidio: Roma e il mondo: Coloquio with J. D. Durand and R. Ladous* (Cinisello Balsamo, 1997), 5–8.

43. Pietro Rossano, *Vangelo in periferia,* in *Memoria* 1 (1988): 50.

44. Ibid.

45. A. Riccardi, "I perché di un libro," in ibid., 54.

46. Ibid., 55.

47. Ugo Poletti, "Tutto il mondo è la mia casa," on the twentieth anniversity of the founding of Sant'Egidio, in *Memoria* 1 (1988): 6.

48. A. Riccardi, "Come a Greccio, per avvicinare Gesù a tanta gente lontana," in *Memoria* 9 (1994–95): 6.

Conclusion

1. H. M. Enzensberger, *Prospettive sulla guerra* [Perspectives on civil war] (Turin, 1994).

2. A. Riccardi, "Le 'pesti' della città," *La Nostra Assemblea* 1 (1984): 8.

3. Antonio Spadaro, "Wake Up the World: Conversations with Pope Francis about Religious Life," in *La Civiltā Cattolica* 165, no. 1, trans. Donald Maldari, SJ (2014): 3.

4. Ibid.